MAN ALONE
COOK BOOK

In the same series

How To Boil An Egg – Simple Cookery For One
Microwave Recipes For One
No Meat For Me, Please!

Where to find *Right Way*

Elliot *Right Way* take pride in our editorial quality, accuracy and value-for-money. Booksellers everywhere can rapidly obtain any *Right Way* book for you. If you have been particularly pleased with any one title, do please mention this to your bookseller as personal recommendation helps us enormously.

Please send to the address on the back of the title page opposite, a stamped, self-addressed envelope if you would like a copy of our *free catalogue*. Alternatively, you may wish to browse through our extensive range of informative titles arranged by subject on the Internet at **www.right-way.co.uk**

We welcome views and suggestions from readers as well as from prospective authors; do please write to us or e-mail: **info@right-way.co.uk**

MAN ALONE COOK BOOK

Don Tibbenham

RIGHT WAY

Typeset in 11 on 12pt Times.

Printed and bound in Great Britain by Cox & Wyman Ltd., Reading, Berkshire.

The *Right Way* series is published by Elliot Right Way Books, Brighton Road, Lower Kingswood, Tadworth, Surrey, KT20 6TD, U.K. For information about our company and the other books we publish, visit our website at www.right-way.co.uk

CONTENTS

INTRODUCTION

This cook book is for all men who live on their own. It is for students as well as for those who have to move away for work and are on their own for the first time. Because men are living longer, a large number suddenly find they are alone: after thirty-five or forty years of marriage, their wife dies and their children have moved away, leaving the man to fend for himself. Men much younger may have divorced or separated or found they are left with youngsters while their wives are in hospital. Others have remained bachelors, live alone in a flat and like to do a spot of cooking.

There are so many things to know when you first start cooking that I decided to jot them all down in a simple and readable way, with a few entertaining cartoon sketches.

Fortunately today there is a lot of prepared and precooked food available so that one can eat quite well with very little trouble, but it can be expensive and become tedious. How much nicer to be able to make a fresh omelette or buy and cook some fresh fish, chicken breasts or meat!

I am alone, with a family miles away, and I have had to start a new life. I did cook as a bachelor, but that was some years ago and conditions have changed. This cook book will, I hope, assist others caught in a similar position, as well as young men starting out in life on their own.

Most of the recipes are for one but often they can be

multiplied up to feed two or three people. Where adjustments to the ingredients have to be made, this is clearly stated. I have also included a short section containing six recipes which are special but simple to make when you wish to entertain a particular guest.

I wish to make it quite clear that the measurements I give are as accurate as possible, but a little over or under will make no real difference. After a few days or weeks you will not need to weigh everything, that is why I use spoons and cups in measurements.

1

TO START

You have electricity or gas in your kitchen or you may
have both. You will probably have a microwave as well.
All this equipment affects the food you buy and the way
you do your cooking.

Your First Visit to the Shops
Superstores and even small shops have a wide range of
frozen foods, many pre-cooked and ready for use. Some
must be thoroughly defrosted, while others can go straight
into the oven or under the grill. If you are not sure, find a
member of the staff to advise you. Most are extremely
helpful people and sympathetic to your problems.

It is essential to read carefully the wording on the packs
before you buy. In many cases the text is so small that it
would be difficult for the elderly to read, but you must
make sure you understand the instructions.

Look at the dates on the packs. They usually include
'Display Until . . .' and 'Use by . . .', 'Keep Refriger-
ated'. If the product can be frozen, it will be clearly stated
on the pack, but in most cases it will say, 'Use within one
month'. Some products can be defrosted and eaten cold,
but this will be clearly stated on them.

One problem you will find is that the majority of
packed foods serve two to four people. In some cases you

can split the products in half and repack in freezer bags to use at different times. This is easiest with items like fish cakes where you can remove one and leave the others sealed for a later date.

Conversion Tables
All measurements are approximate.

Grams to Ounces		*Centimetres to Inches*	
15g	= ½ oz	1cm	= ½"
25g	= 1 oz	2.5cm	= 1"
40g	= 1½ oz	4cm	= 1½"
50g	= 2 oz	5cm	= 2"
65g	= 2½ oz	7.5cm	= 3"
75g	= 3 oz	10cm	= 4"
90g	= 3½ oz	12.5cm	= 5"
100g	= 4 oz (¼ lb)	15cm	= 6"
120g	= 4½ oz	18cm	= 7"
150g	= 5 oz	20cm	= 8"

165g = 5½ oz
175g = 6 oz
185g = 6½ oz
200g = 7 oz
225g = 8 oz (½ lb)
250g = 9 oz
300g = 10 oz
350g = 12 oz (¾ lb)
400g = 14 oz
450g = 16 oz (1 lb)

23cm = 9″
25cm = 10″
28cm = 11″
30cm = 12″

Litres to Pints
25ml = 1 fl oz
50ml = 2 fl oz
85ml = 3 fl oz
120ml = 4 fl oz
150ml = 5 fl oz (¼ pint)
175ml = 6 fl oz
200ml = 7 fl oz
250ml = 8 fl oz
300ml = 10 fl oz (½ pint)
450ml = 15 fl oz (¾ pint)
600ml = 20 fl oz (1 pint)

Oven Temperatures

Gas	Fahrenheit	Centigrade
Low – will warm plates		
1	275°F	140°C
2	300°F	150°C
3	325°F	170°C
4	350°F	180°C
5	375°F	190°C
6	400°F	200°C
7	425°F	220°C
8	450°F	230°C
9	475°F	240°C

Useful Measurements

All cookery books meticulously give imperial and metric
weights and measures for the ingredients in their recipes.
They rarely use spoons and cups, yet few chefs weigh
everything. They use spoons, cups and even a knife. I find
it easier and accurate enough to do as the chefs do.
Therefore, because accurate measurements are not essential in my recipes, I give quantities in this simple way
wherever possible.

APPLES
Cooking
(Bramley's)   Average weight per apple = 175g/6 oz
Eating (Cox's)   Average weight per apple = 150g/5 oz

BUTTER
For all the following measurements one needs butter at room temperature (not straight from the fridge). To calculate the weight I scoop a spoonful of butter and make it level with a knife, or leave it piled up for a heaped spoonful.

1 level dessertspn	= 10g/¼ oz
1 heaped dessertspn	= 15g/½ oz
2 heaped dessertspns	= 25g/1 oz
1 level tablespn	= 25g/1 oz

BREADCRUMBS	1 level tablespn	= 15g/½ oz
(from packet)	2 level tablespns	= 25g/1 oz
	½ cup	= 25g/1 oz

CHEESE (Cheddar) 1 tablespn (grated) = 25g/1 oz

DATES (stoned)   6 dates   = 25g/1 oz

FLOUR	2 heaped dessertspns	= 25g/1oz
	1 heaped tablespn	= 25g/1oz

MILK	1 fairly full cup	
	(about ⅔ of a cup)	= 150ml/¼ pint
	1 tablespn	= $\frac{1}{12}$ of a cup

(There is no need to measure milk for small quantities.)

RICE	1 heaped tablespn	= 25g/1 oz
	2 heaped dessertspns	= 25g/1 oz

SUGAR	1 heaped dessertspn	= 15g/½ oz
	2 heaped dessertspns	= 25g/1 oz
SULTANAS	2 heaped dessertspns	= 25g/1 oz
ONIONS (medium)	Average weight per onion	= 100g/4 oz
WATER	1 fairly full cup	= 150ml/¼ pint
	1 tablespn	= $^1/_{12}$ cup

Things You Want to Know

The simple things you want to know are rarely included in the highly illustrated cookery books on sale today which is why this book has been prepared. Of course, you may have a sister, a daughter or a female friend to telephone

for advice who may even be able to pop round and help! But more likely she either won't be in or won't know the answers to your queries. In that event, my book should be able to help.

BREAD
Do you select a white split tin, a farmhouse or a sandwich loaf?

Obviously it is much cheaper to buy a large loaf, but you realise it will last too long because at mid-day you will probably have sandwiches in the office or in the local with friends. So, if you have a freezer, why not cut a large loaf in half and freeze the half not needed for a few days? Bread will keep for up to six months in the freezer. If you wish to thaw out the whole loaf, leave it in its packet; it will take about four hours to thaw.

If you buy a ready sliced loaf, you can freeze it and just take out a slice at a time and put it straight into the toaster.

BUTTER
Should you use salted or unsalted?

It doesn't matter, but unsalted is best for cooking so that you can add salt as required by the recipe. Most chefs use unsalted and that is what I have used in all my recipes here.

EGGS
How do you separate the yolk from the white?

This isn't easy the first time you do it. Here is the best way:

Crack the egg sharply but gently against the edge of a basin. Put your left thumb in the crack, prise open the shell so that the yolk is in the right half of the shell.

Do this over the basin and most of the white will pour out into the basin.

Tip the yolk from the right-hand half of the shell into the left-hand half and any white left behind should fall into the basin. Now place the yolk into another basin for use when required.

If you have to separate two eggs, it is advisable to carry out the manoeuvre over another basin as you may have the misfortune to break the yolk. A tricky job, but practice makes perfect!

FISH
How do you butter fish ready for cooking?

Your recipe says 'dab with knobs of butter'. Have you tried? It either sticks to the knife/fork or your finger and will not stick to the fish. The only way is to hold the knob of butter on a knife over the fish and push it off with the tip of another knife so that it drops onto the fish. Otherwise you have to melt the butter and spread it on which doesn't produce the same result.

How long can you keep fresh fish?

Up to two days in a cool place, but three to four days in the refrigerator. Correctly packed in freezer bags which exclude as much air as possible, it can be kept in the freezer for up to three months and can be cooked directly from frozen.

ONIONS
If you only use half an onion, can you keep the other half?

Yes, for seven to ten days if you leave it in its skin, put it in a brown paper bag and keep it in a cold place.

POTATOES
How should you keep them?

Never leave them exposed to light as it will turn them green. So put them into a brown paper bag in a cool, dark place where they should keep well for up to ten or fourteen days.

If you boil too many, you can put the spare ones on a plate, covered, in the refrigerator until the next day when you can serve them cold with a salad.

PUDDINGS
What can I do with left-over puddings?

Most puddings (including rice pudding) can be wrapped when cold and kept in the freezer for up to three months. When I make a baked rice pudding, I use the left-overs within two days after adding a little more milk (about a dessertspoon) and reheating it thoroughly on gas 4 (350°F/ 180°C) until it is hot (which takes about 20 minutes). I then add a spoonful or two of jam before serving.

SANDWICHES
Can they be made a day before use?

Yes, if kept in a covered container in the fridge. If made with bread that is just a day old, are well buttered and have a range of fillings other than hard boiled eggs, they can be kept in polythene bags in the freezer for a month or six weeks. But they will take three or four hours to thaw out.

TINNED FOODS

Vegetables such as carrots, peas and beans, as well as stand-bys like ravioli and spaghetti, are now available in various sizes, but if you buy the standard size you may only use half. *Can you keep the remainder for another day?* Yes. If you cover the top of the tin firmly (for example, with cling film) it will keep for two or three days in the refrigerator and be all right for cooking.

TOMATOES
What is the best way to peel a tomato?

Fill a large cup with boiling water and drop in the tomato. Leave it for 2 or 3 minutes depending on size, pour off the water and fill the cup with cold water. Take out the tomato, prick it with a sharp knife and you will be able to pull off the skin easily.

VEGETABLES

Many fresh vegetables (for example, carrots, French beans and parsnips) can be cooked in the same water as potatoes, although not for the same length of time. I like the flavour which onions and leeks give to potatoes when they are cooked together.

Frozen Food

There is a great deal to learn about the use of the freezer, particularly concerning whether vegetables, fruit, meat, fish and cheese should be frozen fresh or cooked. A comprehensive instruction book is essential. You should be able to buy one at your local bookshop. All I can do here is to give you a few useful comments and tips on everyday items.

You should keep a stock of small, medium and large freezer bags and two or three sizes of lidded plastic containers for storing the various items.

BREAD

You will be wise to keep a supply of bread (brown and/or white) in the freezer. See page 14.

FISH

Must be frozen absolutely fresh and must be thoroughly sealed. See page 15.

LEFT-OVERS

Cooking for yourself you will sometimes have left-overs. Most items, such as stews, casseroles, sausages, fish pies, rice pudding and bread and butter pudding, can be kept for two or three days in a cool place or the fridge. I never keep left-overs in the freezer because I never make enough.

Stews can of course be made in quantity, then frozen in

one-portion containers and kept for up to four or five months.

MEAT

Fresh meat can be frozen but must be thoroughly sealed.

POULTRY

If poultry is bought frozen, place it immediately in a freezer shopping bag and as soon as you reach home put into the freezer. Defrosting details will be given on the wrapper; depending on size, this may take up to 24 hours.

VEGETABLES

Most can be frozen fresh but some need blanching (placing in hot water and boiling for 1–2 minutes, then plunging into cold water until cold), then placing in a freezer bag. The list of vegetables which you can freeze is too long to include here; you need to refer to a freezer book.

I find potatoes are a nuisance to peel in small quantities so I prepare and cook more than I need. Those not required are taken from the water, tossed in butter, cooled in the fridge and then frozen for future use in polythene bags or freezer cartons. They will keep for up to three months. Then thaw and re-heat them in a little butter for 5–8 minutes.

Kitchen Utensils and Equipment

You will require a variety of items for even the minimum of cooking. The list I have prepared should cover your immediate needs. In time as you become more experienced you will want to add to the list.

Basins. A small 12.5cm (5″) diameter basin in which you can beat eggs and mixes of ingredients. Another slightly larger, say, 15cm (6″) diameter basin for puddings and heating left-overs. I suggest you buy ones made of oven-proof glass.

Chopping board. Buy a decent size, say 35cm by 25cm (14″ by 10″). This should meet most requirements.

Cling film; aluminium foil; freezer bags and *plastic lidded boxes* in one or two sizes.

Colander for washing vegetables.

Fish slice for lifting fried eggs and fish from your pan.

Forks. You need one or two with heat-proof handles.

Frying pans. One about 21cm (8½″) in diameter by 5cm (2″) deep for frying, and another shallow non-stick pan about 25cm (10″) in diameter, but only 2.5cm (1″) deep, for making omelettes and pancakes.

Grater. This is a standard piece of equipment usually about 15cm (6″) tall by 5cm (2″) wide on the narrow side, with an assortment of grating holes or slots.

Glass jug for measuring, marked in pints, litres or cups.

Electric kettle. I prefer the modern upright ones with visible outside measurements.

Knives. You will need a variety, all with wood or plastic handles:

6.5cm (2½″) with short sharp blade with a point for peeling spuds, etc.

8.5cm (3½″) with a scalloped sharp blade.

10cm (4″), sharp, with a point for cutting meat, poultry, etc.

17.5cm (7″) butcher's knife.

20cm (8″) bread knife with a serrated blade.

Masher. Round metal one (or plastic if using a non-stick pan) about 7.5cm (3″) in diameter with a strong handle, for mashing potatoes, etc.

Electric mixer or food processor.

Oven gloves. Dishes get very hot in the oven or on the hob so make sure you use a good pair of oven gloves.

Pie dishes. Oval with a rim, of 550ml (1 pint) size, about 20cm (8″) long by 6.5cm (2½″) deep, and oven-proof of course, for making rice puddings, pies, etc. You may find it useful to have a slightly smaller pie dish as well.

Roasting tins. A handy size for the man alone is a non-stick metal tin about 20cm (8″) square, but sooner or later you will want a larger one.

Rolling pin. In due course you will need a rolling pin for rolling pastry and for beating meat thin. Buy one not less than 40.5cm (16″) long.

Saucepans. Small non-stick one for milk, etc., about 12.5cm (5″) in diameter. A medium one with a lid, about 15cm (6″) in diameter by 10cm (4″) deep. A large one with a lid, about 23cm (9″) in diameter and 10cm (4″) deep.

Instead of using the medium and large ones, you could obtain a triple saucepan which has two pans and a steamer in which you can cook a number of items at the same time. Some pre-cooked foods such as puddings need steaming, so it is a useful piece of equipment to have.

Spoons, including a slotted spoon for lifting vegetables, like peas, from a pan of water so that the water is left behind in the pan.

Stew pot. There are many types available. I use an earthenware pot with a lid, about 16cm (6½″) at the base and 17.5cm (7″) at the top. Oven-proof of course.

Scales. A small set clearly marked with ounces and grams.

Scissors. A good pair of kitchen scissors with a plastic handle is essential. Buy one you can hang on the wall.

Sieves. You need one about 15cm (6″) in diameter which you can hang on the wall near the scissors.

Spoons. One non-metal spoon is needed when using non-stick pans, and a metal tablespoon is needed for general cooking use. Also required is a soup ladle with a wooden handle and a 2.5cm (1″) wide metal spatula with a wooden handle.

Tin opener.
Electric toaster.

Sandwich toaster. Left-over meals, asparagus, cheese, chicken, prawns, fish and fruit can be used as fillings and served hot. I would not be without mine.

2

TIME TO THINK OF FOOD

Now you have the equipment you need, it is a good idea to plan what you think you would like to eat for the week ahead.

A good start is to prepare a menu. I have created one for your first week to get you thinking along the right lines. It consists of a mixture of ready-prepared dishes and simple recipes you can cook at home. It will help you on your first venture into buying and cooking food, but you may, of course, wish to alter it as the days pass and buy different pre-cooked meals from those I suggest.

Menu for Your First Week

	LUNCH	DINNER
Monday	Soup (e.g. tin of tomato) Cheese sandwiches with pickle	Bought Salmon Cumberland Pie Rice Pudding (page 140)
Tuesday	Slice of tongue Carrot Salad (page 62) Bottle of Guinness	Sausage and mashed potatoes with mushrooms (page 107) Prunes with cream
Wednesday	Lunch out at pub, restaurant or snacks at work	Poached eggs (page 38) on baked beans on toast Cake and coffee
Thursday	Tongue sandwiches Cheese and biscuits Cox's apple	Bought pre-cooked Steak Pie with carrots Cold Rice Pudding from Monday (re-heated if you prefer)
Friday	Smoked ham with a bought mixed salad French roll and butter	Skate au Beurre (page 89) with boiled potatoes Bought Treacle Pudding
Saturday	Sardines on toast Coffee and chocolate biscuits	Steak and Kidney Casserole* (page 99) with boiled potatoes Strawberry ice cream cornet
Sunday	Ham sandwiches with mixed salad (from Friday) Dates (stoned in packet)	Bought ready-to-cook Chicken in Pastry with potatoes and French beans Glass of red wine Banana mashed with cream

*Saturday's casserole should be made large enough for three meals. The surplus when cold can be placed into two separate plastic boxes and frozen for up to four months for future use.

Following a Recipe

Even the simplest recipe should be carefully read so that you can check that you have all the ingredients in stock. If items are in the freezer, make sure you take them out in advance so that they are able to defrost properly. You should also assess the preparation time given in the recipe to ensure you get the accompanying vegetables ready on time. Before you start, it makes it easier if you have all the utensils ready at hand. Remember, also, to pre-heat the oven if required; if this is not done, your meal will be delayed and you will be frustrated.

Keeping Things Hot

Plates can be heated in the oven on low. Depending on the oven you have, the top may get warm enough to heat a single plate. An alternative is to place the plates into hot water in the sink for a few minutes, but they will, of course, need drying before use.

Off to the Shops

You have decided roughly what you wish to eat for the next seven days so now you must go to the shops. You may already have a few basics such as salt, pepper, bread, butter, cheese, eggs, etc., but there are probably many other items you will need. Here is a useful guide to what you may want to buy on your first shopping trip. Make up your own list from it, leaving out those foods you don't require.

Basic Store Cupboard Items
Biscuits: biscuits for cheese and chocolate biscuits.
Bread: white and/or brown, as you prefer.
Breakfast cereals: whatever you like.
Butter: salted or unsalted, to taste.

Cake: it's useful to have a cake in store.

Cheese: see page 35.

Chocolate: a tin of drinking chocolate is useful.

Coffee: whatever you like.

Cornflower: to thicken gravy, stews and soups.

Curry powder: mild Madras or to your taste.

Eggs: essential to keep half a dozen.

Fish: tins of sardines, salmon and prawns.

Fruit:

    apples – always handy. Cox's for eating; Bramley's for cooking.

    bananas – very good for you. I like a small one for breakfast.

    lemon – needed for cooking and for making lemon tea.

Gravy: granules or powder.

Herbs: you need a small selection (see page 32).

Marmalade and jam: one or two jars in stock.

Milk: if not delivered, keep a carton of long life.

Mustard powder.

Nutmeg: an important spice in cooking.

Oil: a bottle of extra virgin olive oil and a bottle of sunflower oil which is lighter and cheaper.

Pepper: white, black (for which you will need a pepper mill) and cayenne.

Pickle/chutney: jar of your favourite variety.

Potatoes.

Prunes: a tin or two to eat hot or cold.

Rice: Carolina or a packet of pudding rice; and long grain rice for savoury dishes.

Salt: I prefer to use sea salt for everyday use – for this, you will need a salt mill.

Sauces: Worcestershire. Chilli and garlic is also useful.

Stock cubes: small packets in fish, chicken, beef or vegetable flavours.

Sugar: caster (a fine textured sugar) mixes easily with butter and margarine, and is used on cereals and fruit;

granulated is coarser and is used generally for cooking; demerara (a natural unrefined cane sugar) is crunchy with a distinctive flavour, and is useful for topping puddings and cakes.

Soups: a selection of small tins. An ordinary size will serve two people, but you can always keep half for another day. See page 16.

Tea: there is a wide choice of tea bags.

Tomato: a bottle of sauce and a tube of purée.

Tomatoes: 225g/½ lb, or select what you want and weigh in the shop.

Vinegar: wine vinegar is best.

Frozen Foods

Chicken pieces.

Ice cream: perhaps including Strawberry Ice Cream Cornet as used in Menu 1.

Vegetables: for example, frozen peas, sweetcorn.

Particular Items Required for Menu 1

Baked beans: a small (150g/6 oz) tin.

Carrots: 2 large or, when new, a small bunch.

Cream: I prefer double cream in a small tub.

French beans: a small packet or 225g/½ lb loose.

Ham, smoked: 100g (4 oz).

Mushrooms: about 100g (4 oz).

Nuts.

Onion.

Salad, mixed: some superstores sell mixed salad in packets or you can select what you need from the market. Little Gem lettuce in packets are wonderful; use one stem and keep the other two for 4 or 5 days.

Sardines: about 120g (4–5 oz).

Sausages: 2 or 3 pork ones.

Skate: 100–125g (4–5 oz).

Tongue: 100g (4 oz).

Steak and kidney: 250g (9 oz).
Sultanas.
Turnip.

Ready-prepared Meals
Chicken in Pastry.
Salmon Cumberland Pie.
Steak Pie.
Treacle Pudding.

Another Week Begins

You have survived your first week looking after yourself, using a selection of ready prepared dishes and some home-made food. However, I have no doubt that you will now wish to do some more cooking for yourself.

To help you, I have prepared a plan for your next seven days. Of course, this can be used at any time. You will see that here I suggest you prepare all your own meals and do not rely on any ready-made dishes. It is fun and more enjoyable. All the recipes are simple and carefully described in the book.

Menu for Your Second Week

	LUNCH	DINNER
Monday	Salmon sandwiches in brown bread with sprinkle of cayenne pepper Cox's apple	Boiled Chicken (page 112) with potatoes, French beans Chocolate ice cream and biscuits
Tuesday	Oxtail soup (tinned) Stilton cheese and biscuits Glass of red wine	Scrambled Eggs on Toast (page 42) Fruit cake and coffee
Wednesday	Cold chicken (from Monday) and salad with boiled potatoes or French bread and butter	Poached Cod (page 74) with a tin of new potatoes Bread and Butter Pudding (page 138)
Thursday	Ham sandwiches Cheese and biscuits if required Coffee	Steak Casserole (last week's) with boiled potatoes Ice cream Glass of red wine
Friday	Ravioli (tinned), bread and butter Bottle of Guinness	Poached Smoked Haddock (page 80) Bread and Butter Pudding (cold from Wednesday)
Saturday	Cup of soup from packet Tongue sandwich	Chicken Madras (page 119) with boiled rice Banana and cream
Sunday	Hot cheese sandwich made in a sandwich toaster Glass of beer	Sweet and Sour Lamb Chops (page 101) Apple or mixed fruit or bought tartlets

Cooking in Earnest Begins

You have stocked up, you know where everything is and you have already started cooking for yourself, so this is where I want to make a few more general comments.

Remember that no one becomes an expert cook overnight so please don't be discouraged if one of your meals isn't as successful as you might have hoped.

As you will see from the recipes I have, wherever possible, included the measurements in spoons and cups as well as weights and measures. Even weights are only a fairly general guide but I am sure you will soon stop measuring every drop of milk or pat of butter. It is a waste of time.

For example, under Scrambled Eggs, I suggest you use a dessertspoon of milk. But this really depends on how you like your scrambled egg, what size egg you buy, and whether it is fresh or not. These things can only be perfected by experience and your special likings.

As you progress with your cooking, you will find that most fish, poultry and meats can be poached, fried, baked, boiled or grilled and it is the variety of ingredients and the sauces which accompany the basic food that makes all the difference to the taste and the appearance. See page 129 for useful sauces and garnishes.

3

USEFUL INFORMATION

Glossary of Cooking Terms

BASTE: To spoon hot melted fat, butter or oil over meat or fish in a frying pan or baking tin to moisten it and assist the cooking.

BEAT: To use a fork or spoon in sharp movements to turn ingredients into a paste or froth. For example, you beat an egg.

BLANCH: To prepare vegetables or fruit for the freezer by placing them in boiling water for 1–2 minutes, then plunging them into cold water to cool them.

BOIL: To cook ingredients in water or other liquid at approximately 100°C/212°F so that the liquid bubbles all the time.

BRAISE: To stew gently in a buttered pan in the oven with the lid on, usually for about 15 minutes.

CHOP: To cut into small pieces, usually on a chopping board.

COAT: To cover an item completely with something, such as to coat fish or meat in flour or in breadcrumbs, or in a beaten egg or in a sauce.

DICE: To cut into small even-sized pieces.

DISSOLVE: This is when an ingredient has to be dissolved before being added to other ingredients, such as a stock cube in water or wine.

FRY: To cook on the hob in a pan of oil, butter or fat at a high temperature.

GLAZE: To brush an item with a beaten egg or milk to give a shiny surface to the cooked item.

GREASE: To rub the surface of a dish or pan with butter or margarine (to prevent the cooked food sticking to it), often by using a piece of butter or margarine paper. I usually do it with a finger.

MARINATE: To soak fish or meat in a flavouring before cooking, often for an hour or longer, in order to enhance the taste and tenderness.

MASH: To use a kitchen masher, fork or food processor to create a smooth paste, such as with potatoes.

MINCE: This is usually done with a food mixer so that the food comes out very thinly cut.

PAR BOIL: To partly cook. This is done to vegetables by placing them into boiling water for a few minutes until partly cooked but still quite firm.

REDUCE: To boil a liquid to reduce the volume and enhance the strength of the flavour. Often done with a wine sauce.

SAUTÉ: To toss in butter or fat in a pan on a hot hob to prevent sticking or burning, especially to seal the juices in meat before grilling or stewing.

SHRED: To slice vegetables, such as cabbage, into thin strands. Can be done in a food processor.

SIMMER: To cook just below boiling so that the liquid only bubbles occasionally.

STEAM: Boiled vegetables can be soft and tasteless if over cooked. It is best to steam them in a double saucepan so that the vegetables are cooked in the steam and they retain the flavour which is often lost in boiling.

ZEST: The outer layer of the skin of citrus fruits such as oranges and lemons.

Herbs

Here is a list of the herbs required in many of the dishes outlined in this book. Most can be bought in powder form for easy use. I have twenty-four herbs in my kitchen.

CHERVIL is one of the herbs in the French *fines herbs* mixture. It has a delicate flavour of anise. Useful to add to sauces and some soups.

CHIVES has a mild onion flavour. A very useful herb which can be used to enhance salads when you don't want to use onions.

DILL has a sweetness with an aromatic sharpness with a caraway flavour. It is good for digestion and very useful.

FENNEL is a very tall plant with a white bulbous base. It

can be cooked in slices, especially for use with oily types of fish, but can also be cut small and used in salads. It has a strong anise flavour.

GARLIC is becoming increasingly popular to add to sauces to give them zest. The bulb is made up of small cloves which can be finely cut or squeezed to add to stews. It has medicinal properties but it does leave an unmistakable odour on the breath. It is available as garlic granules but these are not as good as using the individual cloves.

HORSERADISH has a very strong mustardy flavour and is mainly useful in cold sauces.

MINT grows profusely. New potatoes are improved when boiled with a sprig of it. Also served with lamb.

ROSEMARY is a very fragrant herb and mixes well with other herbs. Rarely used on its own.

TARRAGON is used a great deal in French cooking. Has a superb flavour for enhancing sauces.

THYME has a lemon scent and is an essential item.

Spices

Like herbs, these play an important part in the enjoyment of food. It is a pity that so few people who cook know how or when to use either herbs or spices. You will find a wide selection in most stores which are worth experimenting with.

ALMOND essence. Although this is not a spice, I include it here because it has many uses in flavouring certain dishes such as white fish or sprinkled on toast with an egg.

CARDAMOM seeds (also available in ground form) have a strong aromatic flavour. Used in curries and rice dishes, etc.

CAYENNE is a red hot pepper, used sparingly in many dishes.

CINNAMON powder (or sticks) is spicy and sweet. Used in cooking fruits and with poultry and meats.

CLOVES can be used whole or ground. An important spice with a strong piquant flavour.

CORIANDER is a mixture of flavours with a touch of anise. Useful in stews and meat dishes.

GINGER with its distinctive hot flavour can add a 'kick' to quite ordinary foods. Popular in cakes, biscuits and sweets.

NUTMEG is available in powder form and in small nuts which can be grated over milk puddings, vegetables and fish dishes. Aromatic with a strong bitter-sweet flavour. A great favourite of mine.

PEPPER is an essential in almost everything. Black pepper is best used from a pepper mill, although it is also available in powder form.

SESAME seeds have a nutty flavour and are used scattered over bread, cakes and pastries. Nice sprinkled over salad.

VANILLA is a pale essence with a unique and sweet flavour. Used in cakes, custards and sauces.

Cheeses

British Cheeses

The following British cheeses are the most popular, although they do vary in their quality and maturity. The choice of cheese is very much a personal taste. All the ones I mention can be kept in the refrigerator for days and even weeks if kept in polythene boxes or bags. It is better to take out of the fridge an hour or two before use. Hard cheese can be kept in the freezer for up to six months but will need thawing overnight.

CHEDDAR. Most is factory made and reasonably priced. I prefer Farmhouse Cheddar: it has a fuller but not too strong flavour and keeps longer. Very useful for cooking.

CHESHIRE is a medium-hard red and white cheese.

DOUBLE GLOUCESTER has a mellow delicate flavour with a close crumbly texture.

DUNLOP is a superb Scottish cheese similar to Cheddar but more moist. You will probably only find it in specialist cheese shops. There are of course a number of other delightful Scottish cheeses.

STILTON is a double cream semi-hard blue-veined cheese. It is my favourite and it is most enjoyable eaten with a glass of port.

WENSLEYDALE. A crumbly white cheese, delicious with a shap-flavoured English apple.

Continental Cheeses

There is a vast selection so I can only comment on a few of the most popular ones which are particularly useful for mid-day snacks.

BRIE is a delightful French farmhouse soft cheese which is made in many varieties. It should not be kept too long, preferably eaten within a day or two of purchase.

CAMBOZOLA. A soft, blue-veined German cheese, good with sliced banana and toast.

CAMEMBERT is a very popular French soft white cheese which if kept for any length of time develops a very strong smell. Best to eat it while it is firm and fresh.

DANISH BLUE is well veined and in my opinion rather salty. It is an acquired taste. Can be used in cooking occasionally.

EDAM is a dark yellow round Dutch cheese with a red outside skin. A good solid cheese to eat with pickles.

GORGONZOLA is an Italian semi-hard blue-veined cheese, tasty eaten with biscuits and a glass or two of Valpolicella (a dry red wine from Northern Italy).

GOUDA is another well known Dutch cheese similar to Edam in taste and texture.

GRUYÈRE is a cooked hard cheese riddled with holes, made in Switzerland. A useful cheese for cooking.

PARMESAN is a very hard cheese and is the best for grating and cooking. No chef would be without it. It is the perfect partner for pasta dishes.

4

EGGS

An important food, both nutritious and versatile. Handy for quick snacks, as well as an important ingredient in many recipes. Available in sizes from 1 (large) to 6 (small).

BOILED EGGS

Use eggs at room temperature; don't take them straight from the fridge as they may crack.

Put enough water in a saucepan to cover the egg(s) and bring to the boil, then lower the egg(s) into the water using a large spoon to prevent the egg(s) cracking on the bottom. A little salt and a teaspoon of vinegar added to the water should stop any egg leaking out if there is a slight crack.

Simmer the eggs gently for the following times according to how you like your eggs:

3 minutes for soft
4 minutes for medium-soft
5 minutes for a well-set white
6–7 minutes for hard.

When cooked, place the egg into an egg-cup, pointed

end on top, and gently crack the top to prevent further cooking.

If you wish to use a cold, hard boiled egg for salads, etc., then it should be cooked for 10 minutes and then cooled in cold water. Hard boiled eggs will keep in their shells in the refrigerator for up to 5 days. Do not freeze them.

POACHED EGGS

I use size 2 or 3. The easiest way to cook them is in an egg poacher, obtainable from most hardware stores, but with this the white can become thick and hard.

Another way is to use an egg or muffin ring which will give a fairly even shape. Pour water into a deep frying pan to just below the top of the ring. Heat on the hob. When the water boils, drop the egg into the ring, either straight from the shell or break it into a cup first and then pour into the ring. Then reduce the heat to a simmer. Use a large spoon to baste the water over the yolk to cook it. I always find some of the white comes over the top or seeps from under the ring which makes it difficult to spoon the water; adding a teaspoon of vinegar in the water will help prevent this if the egg is fresh.

When cooked to your liking, lift the ring and take out the egg with a fish slice, trim off any uneven white and serve on hot, well-buttered toast on a pre-heated plate.

I find the *best* way to poach eggs is to pour a little water into a deep frying pan, add a teaspoon of vinegar, bring to the boil, tip the pan sideways, then gently pour in the egg from a cup. Reduce the heat from boiling and spoon the water over the yolk to cook. This should give you the perfect poached egg which you scoop out onto buttered toast.

For *extra flavour*, spread some yeast extract on the hot,

buttered toast and place the egg on top.

The following are a few ways of quickly making a more substantial meal from a poached egg.

HAM
Place a slice of cold, smoked ham on some buttered toast and then place the hot poached egg on top. In Holland they use a thick slice of buttered bread instead of the toast; this is called a Uitsmijter. It makes an enjoyable change from toast.

BEANS
Open a small tin of baked beans, heat thoroughly and serve them round the poached egg on toast. Make sure the plate is hot and add plenty of pepper and salt.

CHEESE
Spread buttered toast with grated Cheddar cheese and grill until nicely soft. Remove and serve on a hot plate with the poached egg on top.

BUCK RAREBIT

This makes a tasty snack or supper but it does take a little longer. I enjoy mine with a large mug of coffee.

Preparation time: 7 minutes.   Cooking time: 4–6 minutes.

1 level dessertspn/10g/¼ oz butter
2 heaped dessertspns finely grated cheese (Gruyère or Cheddar)
1 teaspn Worcestershire sauce
1 dessertspn milk
½ teaspn mustard powder
1 thick slice of white bread
1 egg

Soften the butter in a bowl by stirring it with a fork. Add the cheese to the butter. Pour in the Worcestershire sauce and the milk. Sprinkle over the mustard powder and mix well.

Toast and butter the bread, and heat a plate in the oven on low. Poach the egg. While this is cooking, spread the cheese mixture on the buttered toast and place under a hot grill for 3 or 4 minutes, until the cheese turns nicely brown.

Remove from the grill and place the poached egg on top. Eat while hot, served on the hot plate.

HAM AND EGG CROÛTES

Preparation time: 10 minutes. *Cooking time: 20 minutes.*

2 slices of white bread (large loaf)
1 small (50g/2 oz) onion
1 heaped dessertspn/15g/½ oz butter
1 dessertspn sunflower oil
1 dessertspn chilli and garlic sauce
Seasoning: salt and pepper
2 eggs
2 slices of smoked ham

First, cut 2 slices of bread each about 0.5cm (⅜″) thick, then cut a large circle out of each slice. (See page 135.)

Next, peel and slice the onion and cut it into smallish pieces.

In a frying pan, put the butter and oil, heat over a moderate heat and add the chopped onion. Fry until soft and golden brown (about 8 minutes), then push to one side. Pour in the chilli and garlic sauce, add the seasoning, then mix with the fat and place the circles of bread in the pan. Fry both sides of the bread until they become brown and crispy. If all the butter and liquid is absorbed, you may need a little more butter to ensure the bread is nicely crispy.

Take out and drain on absorbent paper, then remove to a hot plate and cover both with the softened onion pieces. Cover the plate or keep in a warm oven while you poach the eggs (see page 38).

Fold a slice of ham onto each onioned croûte, then place the poached eggs on top and your meal is ready.

SCRAMBLED EGGS

Preparation time: 6 minutes.   Cooking time: 7–8 minutes.

2 eggs
Seasoning: salt and pepper
1 dessertspn milk
1 heaped dessertspn/15g/½ oz butter

I prefer to make this in a deepish saucepan 16.5cm (6½″) in diameter by about 7.5cm (3″) deep, and preferably a non-stick one as a saucepan used for scrambling is a nuisance to clean.

Break the eggs into a basin, beat with a fork, adding salt and pepper and the small amount of milk.

Melt the butter in the pan, then pour in the beaten eggs mixture and cook over a moderate heat, stirring until it is set nicely. Do not let the eggs get too firm; they should remain soft. Serve on a hot plate or on hot, buttered toast if you prefer.

CURRY FLAVOUR
Stir in a teaspoon of mild curry powder to the mixture before cooking.

FISH
If you have any fish (such as cod or smoked haddock) left over from a previous meal, flake it, add it to the melted butter and heat it before pouring in the egg mixture. Then stir well as before. You only need a heaped tablespoon of the fish flakes.

LUXURY
Use a slice of smoked salmon cut into strips about 5cm (2″) long by, say, 0.5cm (¼″) wide. Place the salmon in the melted butter and pour in the egg mixture and stir until the eggs are nicely cooked but soft.

OTHER FLAVOURS
I like to add 4 finely chopped spring onions or a tablespoon of grated Cheddar cheese to the melted butter. Another alternative is to add a heaped tablespoon of chopped ham and a teaspoon of Worcestershire sauce.

FRIED EGGS AND BACON

This is one of the most popular meals, particularly for breakfast, but the yolk is often broken when the egg is removed from the pan, so use a fish slice for this.

Put a heaped teaspoon of butter in the frying pan over a low heat and add 2 rashers of bacon. Fry to your liking, turning the rashers over once or twice so that both sides are cooked, then move them to one side and break 2 eggs into the hot fat.

Depending on how much fat the bacon contains, you will, I expect, need to add more fat to fry the eggs nicely. I usually add a level dessertspoon each of sunflower oil and butter, and baste the eggs with the extra fat to ensure the yolks are nicely cooked.

I like a slice of fried bread with mine. To do this, you have to take out the eggs and the bacon and keep them on a hot plate, then you can fry the bread in the pan until it is nicely brown and crisp. And if you wish, you can also fry a sliced tomato which only takes 3 minutes.

PLAIN OMELETTE

In spite of what people say, it is not difficult to make an omelette, but to make a perfect one, slightly browned on the underside yet moist in the centre when folded ready to serve, requires a knack based on experience. So don't give up.

The omelette is an important dish because it lends itself to a mass of a variations and gives the man alone an opportunity to use his imagination.

Preparation time: 6 minutes.   *Cooking time: about 10 minutes.*

2 eggs (size 2)
1 tablespn water
Seasoning: salt and pepper
1 heaped dessertspn/15g/½ oz butter – depending on how you like your omelette; more may be necessary

Break the eggs into a basin, beat gently with a fork, adding the water and seasoning to taste.

Heat a non-stick frying pan about 25cm (10″) in diameter over a moderate heat, put in the butter so that it covers the surface of the pan and begins to sizzle. Pour in the eggs, leave for a few seconds, then with a wooden spoon or spatula pull the cooking egg slightly from the sides to allow the mixture to flow out to cook. When nicely set and moist in the middle, fold over roughly a third towards the middle, then when the underside is golden brown fold over the other third.

Use a fish slice to take out the folded omelette and place on a hot plate. Eat with a couple of slices of bread and butter.

FILLINGS

Before folding over the omelette, you can add a variety of fillings onto the creamy moist centre, such as:

2 tablespns/50g/2 oz chopped ham
1 tablespn grated cheese
1 thin slice of smoked salmon, chopped into small pieces
1 teaspn mixed dried herbs (mixed into the beaten egg)

Or almost anything you fancy: chopped tomato, spring onions, cooked chicken or spinach, etc.

EGG FLORENTINE

This is a very popular dish and simple to prepare. Today one is able to buy packets of frozen spinach which saves a great deal of trouble and time. It also means you have plenty of spinach available when required.

Preparation time: 10 minutes.   Cooking time: 10 minutes.

1 egg
2 chunks spinach (from a packet)
1 level dessertspn/10g/¼ oz butter
Seasoning: salt and pepper
3 tablespns white sauce (see page 129)
1 tablespn grated Cheddar or Parmesan cheese

Put the egg into a saucepan of hot water and boil it for 5 minutes so that the white is firm and the yolk remains soft. Then take the egg out and place it in cold water, leave for 8 minutes and then remove the shell carefully so as not to break the egg.

While the egg is cooking, place the frozen chunks of

spinach into a saucepan containing one tablespoon of boiling water for 3 minutes, then drain off the water and press the spinach to remove any excess water.

Next put the butter into the pan with the spinach, season with salt and pepper and mix thoroughly, keeping it warm.

Now make a white sauce as per page 129. When ready (in about 4 minutes), pour all but one dessertspoon of the sauce over the spinach in the pan.

Pre-heat the grill. Grease with butter an oven-proof dish and scoop in the spinach. Make a hollow in the centre of the mixture and place in the egg, then pour over the remainder of the sauce and cover with the grated cheese. Place the dish under the grill and cook for about 3 minutes until nicely brown.

5

SANDWICHES
AND QUICK SNACKS

Everyone knows how to make a sandwich but there are a
few variations which you may find will make a welcome
change. You don't need a sandwich toaster for these
recipes.

TOASTED CHEESE AND HAM SANDWICH

This only takes about 8 minutes to prepare.
Cut 2 slices of bread, spread a thin layer of mustard of
your choice on one slice, cover with a thin slice of
Cheddar cheese (or grated), place a slice of ham on top
(but don't let it stick out of the sides). Cover with the
second slice of bread, press down and butter the outside.
Next, place the sandwich on a non-stick shallow tray
and place it under a hot grill until golden brown. Turn it
over and grill the reverse side the same.

TOASTED CHEESE AND TOMATO
SANDWICH

Similar to Toasted Cheese and Ham (above), but using
tomato ketchup instead of mustard.
Cut or grate the Cheddar cheese and spread it on top of

the ketchup. Push down the second slice of bread on top, butter the outside and grill as before until golden brown (about 3 or 4 minutes on each side). Do not allow it to burn.

Instead of tomato ketchup, you can use chutney; I prefer to use Tropical Fruit and Nut Ketchup which I buy from a shop stocking Indian items.

COLD MEAT SANDWICH

Cut the usual 2 or 4 slices of bread, depending on the size of the loaf, and butter one side of each slice.

Cold roast beef is particularly nice when cut thin and laid on the bottom slice of bread and sprinkled with a few drops of Worcestershire sauce. Then place the second buttered slice on top.

You can of course use cold pork or salt beef. Add pepper and salt to taste and, if you don't like Worcestershire sauce, spread a little mustard on the buttered bread instead.

EGG SANDWICH

This takes a bit longer because the eggs have to be hard boiled (about 8–10 minutes – see page 37). When cooked, take them out of the water, tap them gently and place them into cold water when it will be easy to remove the shells.

Cut the eggs into thin slices and lay them on the bottom slice of buttered white bread, season with pepper and salt and with some paprika to give it an uplift. Cover with the buttered second slice and enjoy it with a cup of hot coffee.

TINNED FISH SANDWICH

Open a tin of sardines, tuna fish or salmon, or use some leftovers of white fish such as cod or fresh haddock.

Mash the fish with a fork, adding a few drops of lemon juice (or chilli and garlic sauce), sprinkle with pepper but not salt. Then spread on one of the buttered slices of bread. Cover with mayonnaise, then place the second slice of buttered bread on top and push down firmly. Cut into quarters and it's ready to eat.

The tinned salmon is my favourite. You can of course use prawns instead if you prefer. Delicious.

HAM SANDWICH PLUS...

A slice of ham between 2 slices of bread and butter is a very dull sandwich. Here is a more interesting one.

Cut 2 thin slices of white bread. Butter them and season with pepper to taste. Lay on a thin slice of smoked ham, cover with 3 heaped teaspoons of salad cream, then sprinkle on top 3 or 4 finely chopped spring onions. Seal with the buttered side of the second slice of bread. Push it down firmly and cut into quarters with a sharp knife.

A nice Cox's apple afterwards completes this enjoyable snack.

FRIED SANDWICH

This makes a pleasant and delectable change from a plain ham sandwich.

Cut and butter 2 medium-thick slices of white bread. Lay on one piece a thin slice of roast or smoked ham to fit the bread, then a layer of Gruyère cheese up to the edges of the bread. Press the second slice of buttered bread down firmly on top.

Heat a heaped dessertspoon/15g/½ oz of butter in a lidded frying pan and place in the sandwich and brown lightly on both sides. Then on the top side sprinkle on a thin layer of grated Gruyère cheese. Put on the lid and continue to heat gently for 2 or 3 minutes to ensure the cheese on top melts slightly. It is then ready to remove and serve.

A strong cup of coffee goes nicely with this.

TONGUE WITH CHEESE

A straightforward tongue sandwich needs no instructions but it is rather boring, so I recommend this variation:

Cut and butter 2 slices of white bread. On one slice fold in a thin slice of tongue, then cover with thin slices of Gruyère cheese and spread over the top 2 teaspoons of mayonnaise. Place on the second slice of buttered bread and you have a nice savoury sandwich.

NUTTY LIVER PÂTÉ

You will probably keep one or two tins of pâté in store for an emergency when you need a quick snack. You can, of course, find a wide selection of pâtés on display in superstores or delicatessens. This recipe makes a nourishing, tasty change from just eating the pâté with a salad.

Preparation time: 5 minutes.

1 slice (100g/4 oz) of liver pâté
3 dessertspns/25g/1 oz walnuts
1 dessertspn whisky

Put the pâté in a basin and loosen with a fork. Chop the walnuts into small pieces, pour them into the basin with the meat, add the whisky, mix well and serve on 2 slices of buttered toast (small loaf size).

FRENCH-STYLE SANDWICHES

Use a French baguette or individual crisp rolls which you
can obtain at many superstores or specialist bread shops.

Split the baguette or rolls lengthwise and remove some
of the soft bread from the centre to leave space in which
to build up one of the following fillings:

HAM AND EGG

Spread one of the open sides of the roll or baguette with
butter and then with a thin layer of French wine mustard.
On top, place a thin slice of ham, next put on a layer of
thin slices of hard boiled egg. Add salt and pepper and
then another layer of ham. Butter the other half of the
roll/baguette and place on top.

SARDINE

Butter both open sides of the roll or baguette and sprinkle
in 3 or 4 finely chopped spring onions.

Open a tin of sardines in tomato sauce, break up 2 or 3
sardines with a fork and push down over the chopped
onions. Pepper well and place the other half of the roll or
baguette on top and it is ready to eat.

HOT SHRIMP OR CRAB

As before, butter both open sides of the roll or baguette,
then put in a layer of finely chopped spring onions.

Open a small jar of shrimp or crab paste and fill up the
bread with a generous layer of the paste of your choice.
Next, cover with a thin layer of grated Gruyère cheese
and a sprinkle of olive oil. Cover with the other buttered
side of the roll/baguette, wrap in foil and place in a heated
oven on gas 2 (300°F/150°C) for about 15 minutes and
serve hot. The cheese will melt and soak into the fish.

There are other variations, including chopped chicken,
onions and mayonnaise, that you might like to try.

GARNISHED EGGS

Serve these for lunch with 2 slices of buttered white bread or, better still, with a crisp French roll sliced and buttered, and perhaps with a glass of light ale to quench your thirst.

Preparation and cooking time: 10–12 minutes.

2 eggs
3 or 4 lettuce leaves
1 dessertspn mayonnaise
Few capers
4 spring onions (finely chopped)
4 anchovies (from a small tin – about 50g/1.75 oz)

The eggs have to be hard boiled (which takes about 10 minutes – see page 37) and you can do this while you are having your breakfast. When cooked, crack them by gently tapping the shells and then place them in cold water when it will be easy to remove the shells.

At lunchtime, place the lettuce leaves on a large dinner plate, cut the eggs in half and arrange them on the lettuce, then pour the mayonnaise over them. Sprinkle the capers and the spring onions over the sauce. Garnish with the anchovies across the tops of the egg halves.

CELERY HEARTS SPICED WITH ANCHOVIES

Another use for part of the tin of anchovies used in the previous recipe. I like a glass of white wine with this and, of course, a few slices of bread and butter.

Preparation time: 5 minutes.

3 or 4 lettuce leaves
397g/14 oz tin of celery hearts
½ small tin (145g/5.1 oz) of peas*
1 dessertspn mayonnaise
1 chopped hard boiled egg
3 or 4 anchovies (from a small tin – about 50g/1.75 oz)

Cover a large dinner plate with the lettuce leaves and place the celery hearts on top. Open the tin of peas into a strainer and drain well (you may only need half of them), then put into a basin, add the mayonnaise and mix together. Pour over the celery hearts and decorate with the egg and the anchovies on top.

*Instead of a tin of peas, you could keep a packet of frozen petit pois in your freezer: take out 2 tablespoons of them, put into boiling water for 2 minutes, remove and use when cold.

6

VEGETABLES

POTATOES

The potato is undoubtedly the most popular vegetable which many people eat every day. It is full of goodness, although most is in the skin. Most potatoes can be well scrubbed and cooked in their skins, but old and warty ones must be peeled. Personally, I always peel all old potatoes.

For storage even for a short time, they should be kept in a cool place in a brown paper bag. The top should be loosely folded to exclude light as this can cause the outsides to turn green. If they are only slightly green, cut off the green area before cooking; otherwise throw away all green potatoes.

BOILED

This is the normal way of cooking. If the potatoes are very old, peel them, cut out the 'eyes' and other damaged parts, then cut them lengthwise and then into half again.

Place them in a saucepan with enough cold water to cover them, add about ½ teaspoon of salt and bring to the boil. Place on the lid and simmer for about 20 minutes. You can test if they are cooked with a kitchen fork: if it goes in well, they are ready. Drain off the water and serve with a sprinkle of freshly chopped parsley or chopped mint.

New Potatoes should not be peeled, but just boiled for about 15 minutes, served with a sprinkling of finely chopped mint.

MASHED

Cook as above. When drained, mash with a kitchen masher, adding a splash or two of milk and a level dessertspoon/10g/¼ oz of butter. Season well with salt and pepper. Serve on a hot plate – remember potatoes cool quickly.

ROAST

Old potatoes should be used for this. Prepare as for boiled, but simmer only for about 6 minutes. Drain off the water and cut into even-sized pieces which you should then place into a roasting tin with dripping from cooked meat or with butter. Cook in a pre-heated oven on gas 7 (425°F/220°C) for 20–25 minutes until nicely brown. Turn them over, baste them and bake for another 20–25 minutes or longer until brown and crisp.

Most people when cooking a joint of meat roast the potatoes in the same dish at the same time as the joint.

BAKED IN THEIR JACKETS

The potatoes must be thoroughly scrubbed and any 'eyes' removed. Cut a deep cross on one side and then place on the centre shelf of the oven, pre-heated on gas 6 (400°F/200°C), and cook for 1–1½ hours, depending on the size.

When cooked, open the cross and put in a good-sized lump of butter or, if you prefer, some sour cream, pepper and salt. If you wish, you can push in 2 finely chopped spring onions to add a little extra flavour.

LYONNAISE

For one large potato you need to peel and slice half a medium-sized onion. Then fry the onion in a dessertspoon of olive oil over a medium heat for about 8 minutes until soft.

The potato should be boiled but slightly under cooked, drained and cut into thin slices, then put into the pan with the cooked onion and fried gently, turning from time to time until both potato and onion are lightly brown. Serve with finely chopped fresh parsley or chopped mint.

CROQUETTES

These require more time but can be well worthwhile if you decide to entertain a friend for dinner.

Season some mashed potatoes with pepper and salt, then mix in most of a beaten egg (leave a small amount for coating later). Make into a smooth paste and divide into sausage-sized shapes, brush the outside with a little of the beaten egg and roll in a saucer of breadcrumbs to form a coating.

Place the croquettes into a frying pan with olive oil and a teaspoon of chilli and garlic sauce. Fry over a moderate heat until crisp and brown when they are ready to serve.

When hard and cold, they can be kept in the freezer for a month or two, then fully thawed and placed into deep fat to heat thoroughly.

SPICED NEW POTATOES

An interesting and spicy way to sauté potatoes; it does involve a little extra work but doesn't take long to cook. This dish can be eaten by itself or you can serve it with lightly poached fish, such as cod or haddock, or with cold or hot chicken.

Preparation time: 8 minutes. Cooking time: 10–15 minutes.

7–8 new potatoes
2 tablespns sunflower oil
1 dessertspn chilli and garlic sauce
2 teaspns cumin
1 teaspn cayenne pepper
1 dessertspn desiccated coconut
1 dessertspn sesame seeds (optional)
1 teaspn garam masala
Sprinkle of nutmeg

Place the potatoes into boiling water and par boil them for 10 minutes, then remove them and cut into halves.

Into a deep frying pan, pour the oil and the chilli and garlic sauce. Heat over a moderate heat until it is nicely hot, then add the cumin and cayenne pepper, stir and then add the halved potatoes. Sauté the potatoes until nicely browned on the cut sides and slightly crisp, then add the coconut (if from a block, crumble it first) and mix it into the liquid. This will take about 10 minutes. Just before the end of that 10 minutes, add the sesame seeds and the garam masala.

Serve the hot potatoes on a hot plate and sprinkle over a little nutmeg.

OTHER VEGETABLES

Most vegetables (including the following) can be kept for 5–7 days in a cool, dark place (a larder if available) or in the vegetable section of the refrigerator.

BEANS

There are many varieties so I will just mention the most popular ones. Fresh beans, such as broad beans and French beans, which are normally cooked to eat with meats, chicken, fish, etc., can also be used cold in salads, but it is best to cut the long French green beans into smallish pieces to mix with other vegetables, such as lettuce, onions, tomatoes, carrots, etc.

BROAD BEANS
These have a short season and are best bought in frozen packets. Cook according to the instructions.

FRENCH BEANS
Available loose or in packets at most superstores. To cook, place into boiling water and boil for 10–15 minutes until tender but not soft or floppy.

RUNNER BEANS
Are quite large and have a limited season. Before cooking, remove the stalk and long stringy bits with a knife, and slice at an angle horizontally. Place in hot water and boil for about 10 minutes.

DRIED BEANS
There is a large family of dried beans and pulses, such as chick peas, flageolets, red kidney beans, etc., which you can keep in your store cupboard for months. They are a

good source of protein and make excellent additions to salads, casseroles and pasta dishes.

To prepare, soak overnight in cold water (enough to cover). When you are ready to do your cooking, you should boil the beans or pulses in fresh water for a few minutes until tender. When cooking red kidney beans, be sure to boil them fiercely for a minimum of 10 minutes to destroy toxins in them, then simmer until tender.

BROCCOLI OR CALABRESE

This vegetable is available most of the year. It needs cutting into moderate-sized portions, then cooking by plunging into salted, boiling water for about 5–6 minutes. Drain well and serve hot. It can also be eaten cold and with salads.

CABBAGE

The most useful for cooking is the white cabbage and most shops will sell you half a white cabbage.

It is best to cut and slice the cabbage before placing it into boiling water for cooking. It should not be over-cooked as its delicate flavour will be destroyed and you will lose its crispness, so cook for about 5 minutes.

Drain thoroughly before serving and toss it in melted butter, salted and peppered.

CABBAGE, BRAISED

This makes an enjoyable change from the straightforward boiled cabbage. Place the cut and sliced cabbage into salted, boiling water for about 8 minutes, drain well and when cool separate the leaves. Put a level dessertspoon/ 10g/¼ oz of butter into a frying pan, when hot add the leaves and braise over a moderate heat for about 3 minutes until the leaves start to brown. Add salt and pepper and serve hot.

BRUSSELS SPROUTS

This is mainly a spring and winter vegetable. They should never be overcooked; they should be crisp but gently soft to retain their delicate flavour. It is preferable to buy the smaller ones as they have a sweeter taste.

Remove any tough stem and discoloured outer leaves, make a cut in the base and cook in salted, boiling water for about 6–7 minutes.

Sprouts are particularly enjoyable if served with skinned and boiled chestnuts which are usually in season at the same time. This is a fiddly job but you can use tinned peeled chestnuts instead.

Another method is to put the cooked sprouts into a pan with a level dessertspoon/10g/¼ oz of butter, some salt and pepper and a sprinkle of nutmeg. Cover with a thin layer of grated cheese (Cheddar or Parmesan) and place under a hot grill for about 3 minutes until lightly brown.

CARROTS

Carrots are available all the year round and can be eaten raw or cooked. They contain vitamin A as well as vitamin C, with plenty of fibre. In early summer they can be bought in bunches when quite small and tender. Only buy them with the tops on so you can make sure they are fresh.

YOUNG SMALL CARROTS
Can be kept for many weeks in the freezer. You should remove the tops, wash the carrots well and leave to dry.

Then pack them closely in a box or bag in the freezer. To cook, boil them for 15 minutes in salted water.

OLD CARROTS
Should be washed and well scrubbed. I prefer to scrape them gently, cut into slices and boil lightly for 15–20 minutes until a fork will enter the slices easily.

As old carrots are always available there is no need to freeze them, but if you do, they will need blanching in boiling water for 3 minutes before being left to cool and sealed in polythene bags.

RAW CARROT SALAD

Preparation time: 7 minutes.

1 large carrot
1 dessertspn olive oil
1 dessertspn sultanas
1 dessertspn chopped nuts
1 teaspn caster sugar
Seasoning: salt and pepper
Squeeze of lemon juice

Clean the carrot and use your grater to reduce the carrot to a heap of small strips into a bowl or basin. Add all the other ingredients and mix thoroughly with a fork. This should give you enough to serve with 2 meals of cold meats, ham, tongue or chicken.

CAULIFLOWER

A very useful and popular vegetable, usually available from June through to the autumn. To cook, separate the florets and place them in boiling water, then cook until tender but remaining firm. About 7–8 minutes should be long enough. The florets can be chopped raw and used in vegetable salads.

CAULIFLOWER AU GRATIN

This is my favourite way of enjoying cauliflower.

Preparation time: 15 minutes.   Cooking time: 20 minutes.

4 or 5 cauliflower florets
1 heaped dessertspn/15g/½ oz butter
Seasoning: salt and cayenne pepper
150ml/¼ pint white sauce (see page 129)
1 tablespn grated Cheddar cheese
25g/1 oz breadcrumbs

Pre-heat the oven on gas 4 (350°F/180°C).

Trim off the outer leaves of the cauliflower and some of the thick stem, and lightly steam or boil the florets for about 5 minutes. Remove and cut into smallish pieces and place into a buttered baking dish. Season well with plenty of cayenne pepper and salt.

Cover with the white sauce, thickened with a tablespoon of the grated cheese. Sprinkle the breadcrumbs over the top and place the dish into the pre-heated oven for 10–15 minutes.

A LITTLE EXTRA
An interesting addition to the cheesy white sauce is to sprinkle in a dessertspoon of finely chopped nuts which can be bought at your local superstore.

COURGETTES

The best ones are of medium size and should be used within about 4 days of purchase. They should be kept in a cool place or in the refrigerator salad section.

Courgettes can be boiled, sautéed or deep fried, always with the skins left on. Clean the outside and nip off the tops and the tails. Cook whole or in thin slices (which most people seem to prefer). Cooking time is short, only 5 or 6 minutes.

You can give your courgettes a little extra flavour by following this simple recipe.

Preparation time: 5 minutes.   Cooking time: 7–8 minutes.

3 medium courgettes
2 level dessertspns/15g/½ oz butter
Seasoning: salt
1 teaspn oregano
1 dessertspn Hot Pepper and Lime Sauce

Clean the courgettes well and cut into 5mm (¼″) slices. Melt the butter in a frying pan, add salt, oregano and the Hot Pepper and Lime Sauce. When nicely hot, add the courgette slices and fry gently for 6 minutes, turning the slices over to prevent burning.

MUSHROOMS

There are many varieties but in my recipes I only include the ordinary flat mushrooms. If I use button mushrooms I say so in the particular recipe, but personally I find them rather tasteless and only suitable in stews.

Many people skin the large mushrooms before chopping, but it is only necessary to wipe the top skin clean. They take about 3–4 minutes to fry in butter.

SAMPHIRE

This is a tasty seaweed with a limited season. Usually sold by weight, often in fish shops.

Place it in boiling water and boil for about 15 minutes so that the succulent flesh can be sucked off the fibrous stems. As enjoyable as eating asparagus – or even better!

SPINACH

This is a popular vegetable. It is usually bought by weight. You must remember it is bulky and reduces considerably when cooked.

Before cooking, remove and discard the stalks. Then place it in about 2.5cm/1″ of boiling water and boil for 2 or 3 minutes. Remove into a sieve, press out surplus water with the back of a spoon before using.

Spinach can be bought frozen in packets so you can just extract the amount you want and keep the remainder in the freezer for another time.

7

RICE AND PASTA

RICE

Rice is a very important item and used increasingly in place of potatoes, especially with spicy Indian and Chinese foods. Many people find it difficult to cook; I must admit it is not easy because it can quickly become soggy with the grains sticking together.

Long grain rice is used for savoury dishes, while short grain rice is used for puddings, such as rice pudding.

If you buy loose packed rice, it is important to wash it thoroughly in cold water to remove excess starch and impurities. The easiest way is to place the rice into a sieve under a running cold tap, giving it a few shakes until the water runs clear.

The safest and best way to cook rice is to put it into a lidded saucepan with double the amount of water: that means for one cup of rice, you need 2 cups of water. Then bring it to the boil, put on the lid and simmer for about 15 minutes. You have to look at it occasionally as rice absorbs water and could easily burn so you will need to stir it from time to time. You may be tempted to add more water but if the rice is cooked and tender it will only make it soggy.

Fortunately today you can buy long grain rice in packets containing single portion sachets of ready-prepared rice which can be cooked in the bag for 20 minutes (see pack instructions). Long grain rice is also available in tins, pre-cooked, which only needs 3 minutes to heat up with a small amount of water. Once the tin is opened, the remainder will only keep in the refrigerator for 2 or 3 days.

There are many other interesting packets of rice on the market such as seasoned and special fried rice. These can accompany a meal or even be eaten as a snack on their own. They only need about 10 minutes to get ready (see instructions on the packs).

Important: cooked rice should not be kept long because it spoils very quickly, especially in hot weather. It may be kept overnight in the refrigerator provided it is cooled as quickly as possible after cooking. Before eating the next day, re-heat it quickly, making sure it is completely hot.

RISOTTO OF KIDNEYS

Preparation time: 10 minutes.   Cooking time: 30 minutes.

4 kidneys
2 heaped dessertspns/25g/1 oz butter
½ onion (sliced)
1 mushroom (finely cut, without stalk)
½ beef stock cube dissolved in ½ cup of water
1 dessertspn tomato purée
½ cup sherry
2 level dessertspns rice (or pasta)
1 tomato (peeled and sliced)
Seasoning: salt and pepper
1 heaped dessertspn grated Parmesan cheese

Pre-heat the oven on gas 4 (350°F/180°C).

Trim the kidneys by cutting them in half and removing the gristle and suet from the centre if not removed before purchase. Heat the butter in a pan over a moderate heat, add the kidneys and lightly brown over the heat for about 3 minutes.

Remove the kidneys onto a hot plate and add the sliced onion and chopped mushroom to the juices. Sauté for 3 minutes. Then add the beef stock, tomato purée, sherry and the rice. Cook slowly until the rice has absorbed the liquid and is tender (about 15 minutes). More stock or water can be added if necessary to avoid over cooking and/or drying out.

Now slice the kidneys and add them to the pan. Also add the tomato and season with salt and pepper.

Pour the mixture into an oven-proof dish. Sprinkle Parmesan over (you can use mature Cheddar if you prefer) and dot with butter. Cook in the pre-heated oven for 10 minutes, then serve.

PASTA

There are many varieties of pasta so I only give a few comments on four of the most used. To cook, place the pasta into boiling water and continue boiling until tender. The individual packets will specify the recommended cooking times.

SPAGHETTI
Long thin sticks. To cook, place the ends into boiling water. As they soften, wind them round the saucepan and continue cooking until tender.

TAGLIATELLE
Narrow flat strips of egg pasta of various flavours, such as verdi (spinach), tomato (orange-coloured) or flavoured with garlic and herbs.

When bought dried they are wound into little nests. Fresh are now widely available in delicatessens or supermarkets.

FARFALLE
Flat pasta in butterfly shapes.

FUSILLI
Spiral pasta that looks like small barley sugar sticks.

TOMATO AND KIDNEY BEAN PASTA

Any pasta can be used in this recipe, but I've chosen fusilli because its spiral shapes hold the sauce better than the more straight-forward shapes.

Preparation time: 8 minutes. Cooking time: 15–20 minutes.

75g/3 oz fusilli pasta
2 tablespns olive oil
¼ teaspn chilli paste
1 teaspn garlic (or 2 crushed garlic cloves)
⅓ cup sliced sundried tomatoes (not fresh tomatoes)
4 chopped spring onions
1 tablespn chopped fresh basil or dried basil
¼ teaspn ground ginger
¼ cup of canned kidney beans
1 dessertspn tomato purée
½ cup water

Heat some water in a saucepan, bring to the boil and add the pasta. Simmer for 15 minutes or until the pasta is tender (*al dente*).

In a deep frying pan, heat the olive oil over a moderate heat. Add the chilli paste, garlic, sundried tomatoes, spring onions, basil, ginger and the beans. Stir fry for 1 minute.

Next add the cooked pasta. Mix the tomato purée in half a cup of water and stir lightly into the pasta, then serve.

SHRIMP PASTA

This recipe makes a really delicious dish. It may sound complicated but it is quite simple and is well worth doing. A crisp green lettuce salad suits it well.

Preparation time: about 15 minutes.   *Cooking time: 30 minutes.*

75g/3 oz small brown shrimps (fresh)
4 tablespns milk
75g/3 oz egg noodles
1 teaspn olive oil
75g/3 oz peeled prawns
2 tablespns cream
Seasoning: salt and pepper

You need fresh shrimps which you must peel. Reserve the shells, heads and tails and put them into a small saucepan, cover with the milk and simmer for 20 minutes, stirring from time to time. It will reduce into a concentrated shrimp flavour.

Put the noodles into a saucepan of boiling water and add the olive oil. Boil for 15 minutes or until tender.

Next, strain the milk to take out the shrimp shells, heads and tails, and return the milk to the saucepan. Then add the peeled shrimps, prawns, cream, salt and pepper, and warm gently.

Strain the noodles and pour the shrimp sauce over them, toss the noodles to coat well with the sauce and serve on a hot plate.

PASTA WITH PESTO

This is a delightful way to eat pasta, although it does mean you have to buy two Italian cheeses, but you should be able to buy them at your superstore or local delicatessen. Your own homemade pesto is infinitely more tasty, but if you are short of time most supermarkets stock a ready-prepared pesto sauce.

Serve on a hot plate with a green salad. I like to use the small compact and crisp Little Gem lettuce which keeps well in the refrigerator.

Preparation time: 8 minutes.   *Cooking time: 10 minutes.*

50g/2 oz Pecorino cheese
25g/1 oz grated Parmesan cheese
1 dessertspn pine kernels
2 sprigs fresh basil (torn into pieces)
1 teaspn garlic granules
1 tablespn olive oil
50-75g/2-3 oz tagliatelle or fusilli pasta

First, prepare the pesto sauce. Put the Pecorino, Parmesan, pine kernels, basil, garlic and olive oil into your food processor. (If you haven't got one, chop the basil, then mix it well with all the other ingredients – except the pasta – with a kitchen fork.)

Next cook the pasta. Put it into boiling water and cook for 7-8 minutes (or as per the instructions on the packet). When it's soft, drain well and return it to a hot pan. Pour over the pesto sauce and stir it well so that the pasta is well coated. Then heat for 3 or 4 minutes before serving.

8

FISH

Fish is a highly nutritious food: as well as protein, it contains valuable vitamins and minerals; white fish is low in fats and carbohydrates.

To make sure the fish you buy is fresh and has not been kept for a long time in a freezer, look at it carefully: the eyes should be bright and outstanding; the flesh firm and should not smell of ammonia.

Most white fish can be pan fried in butter to which you should add a teaspoon of cooking oil to prevent burning. Each portion will take a slightly different cooking time. A fillet of cod or fresh haddock about 75–100g (3–4 oz) in weight needs about 3 minutes on the skin side and 5–8 minutes on the flesh side. You can judge when it is cooked by testing it with a fork: if the flesh flakes easily it is ready.

There is a large variety of fish and there are many different ways of cooking it from frying, poaching, grilling and baking to the preparation of pies and kedgerees. I have restricted myself in this chapter to giving you a few easy and quick methods. If you become an enthusiast, you will need a cookery book devoted entirely to the subject.

The first time I cooked fish I found it rather unpleasantly slippery, but if you give it a good rinse under the cold tap first, it is easier to handle.

POACHED COD

Preparation time: 5 minutes.   Cooking time: 8–10 minutes.

1 heaped dessertspn/15g/½ oz butter
1 90g/3½ oz cod steak (about 2.5cm/1″ thick)
1 tablespn milk
Seasoning: salt and pepper

Smear a little butter on both sides of the fish steak and place it in a frying pan. Add the rest of the butter and the milk, salt and pepper. Bring to the boil, then simmer for 8–10 minutes until cooked. Serve on a hot plate.

The dish can be improved by making a little sauce. Mix a teaspoon of cornflour into half a glass of white wine and stir this into the remainder of the milk in which you poached the fish. Heat and then pour over the fish.

FRIED COD

Serve on a hot plate with a few potatoes.

Preparation time: 6–7 minutes.   Cooking time: 12 minutes.

1 heaped dessertspn/15g/½ oz butter
1 dessertspn sunflower oil
5 or 6 spring onions (finely chopped)
1 level dessertspn plain flour
Seasoning for the flour: salt and pepper
1 90g/3½ oz cod steak (about 2.5cm/1″ thick)
Lemon (just a squeeze)
1 heaped dessertspn chopped parsley

Over a low heat melt the butter in a small frying pan with the oil. Add the chopped onions and cook for about 3 minutes until soft but not browned.

Season the flour with salt and pepper to your liking, then coat both sides of the cod steak with it. Then place the fish into the hot butter, pushing the onions to one side. Sprinkle the cod steak with some lemon juice, then fry it for about 4–5 minutes on each side. Scatter the chopped parsley over the steak and serve.

MINTED COD

A really delicious way to prepare and cook cod. This recipe feeds one person but with a small adjustment it is easy to prepare it for two: you will need 225g–250g/8–9 oz of cod fillet and 2 dessertspoons of oil while the amounts for the other ingredients remain the same.

To save yourself time, when you buy the fillet of cod ask your fishmonger to skin it and cut it into 4 or 5 narrow strips. Do not buy the tail end; you will get more regular slices from the centre of the fillet.

While the fish is cooking, you can boil some new potatoes (page 56) and perhaps cook some French beans (page 59). In season I like to cook some samphire (page 65). Then I serve it all on a hot plate and enjoy it with a glass of red wine.

Preparation time: 10 minutes, plus 1 hour marinating.
Cooking time: 25 minutes.

1 dessertspn chilli and garlic sauce
1 dessertspn sunflower oil
1 teaspn turmeric
½ teaspn coriander
½ teaspn cumin
½ teaspn cayenne pepper
Juice of ½ a lemon
125g/5 oz fillet of cod
1 tablespn chopped mint (I find it easier to use a pair of
    kitchen scissors for this)
1 level dessertspn/10g/¼ oz butter

First, make the marinade for the fish slices. Pour the chilli and garlic sauce into a dish with the sunflower oil, then mix in the turmeric, coriander, cumin, cayenne and lemon juice. Next add the slices of cod and leave for an hour to absorb the flavours, turning them from time to time.

Pre-heat the oven on gas 7 (425°F/220°C). Take the marinated cod strips and roll them in the chopped mint.

Grease well with butter a lidded oven-proof dish and place in the minted fish strips, then gently pour the marinade over the fish. Put on the lid and place the dish on a mid-way shelf of the pre-heated oven and cook for 25 minutes.

BAKED COD PORTUGUESE STYLE

Preparation time: 15 minutes.   Cooking time: 45 minutes.

2 medium-sized potatoes (225g/8 oz)
Seasoning: salt and pepper
1 heaped dessertspn/15g/½ oz butter
1 skinned fillet of cod (100g/4 oz)
4 thin onion slices (well chopped)
2 medium-sized tomatoes (sliced)
½ teaspn garlic granules (or 1 chopped clove)
2 teaspns Worcestershire sauce
1 tablespn milk
1 teaspn cornflour

Pre-heat the oven on gas 6 (400°F/200°C). Peel the potatoes and par boil them in hot, salted water. This will take about 10 minutes as they should not be completely cooked. Remove them and cut them into thin slices.

Grease thoroughly an oven-proof dish with butter and cover the base with a layer of the sliced potatoes (keep half the slices for later use), then place the fillet of cod on top. Sprinkle the onion slices over the cod, then add the sliced tomatoes, with the salt, pepper and garlic. Next cover with a layer of the remaining sliced potatoes, dabbing butter on top.

Mix the Worcestershire sauce with the milk, adding and mixing in the cornflour, then pour it over the top. Then place the dish into the pre-heated oven and cook for 45 minutes.

POLLOCK MORNAY

This is a pleasing fish of the cod family (so you can cook cod in the same way) usually caught in northern waters near Norway. Enjoy with a few new potatoes and a little lettuce salad.

Preparation time: 10 minutes.   *Cooking time: 15 minutes.*

1 level dessertspn/10g/¼ oz butter
1 dessertspn/15g/½ oz flour
¾ cup milk
1 dessertspn olive oil
1 level teaspn mustard powder
Seasoning: salt and pepper
115–125g/4½–5 oz pollock (I prefer the tail end of the fillet)
1 tablespn/25g/1 oz grated Parmesan or Cheddar cheese

First make the mornay sauce. Melt half the butter in a small saucepan over a low heat, sprinkle in the flour, stirring all the time as you add some of the milk over a simmering heat until nicely creamy (about 5 minutes).

Cook the pollock over another heat ring. To do this, you need a frying pan into which you should melt the remaining butter, the olive oil, mustard powder and seasoning. When bubbling, place in the fillet of pollock, skin side down, and simmer for 3 minutes. With a fish slice turn it onto its fleshy side and cook for another 4 minutes, then turn it back to its skin side and cook for another 3 minutes. It helps to baste the flesh with some of the juices using a spoon.

During the final stages of cooking the fish, sprinkle the grated cheese into the sauce and stir it in with the remainder of the milk. Place the fish onto a hot plate and stir the sauce until it is nicely creamy. If too thick, add a spot more milk, then pour over the fish and serve.

SMOKED HADDOCK RAREBIT

A glass of white wine complements this dish.

Preparation time: 12 minutes.   Cooking time: 15 minutes.

2 tablespns grated Cheddar cheese
¼ teaspn mustard powder
1 teaspn Worcestershire sauce
Seasoning: pepper NOT salt
2 tablespns milk
1 tomato
1 tablespn water
100g/4 oz fillet of smoked haddock (I prefer the tail end)
1 thin slice of white bread (small loaf)

Grate the cheese into a bowl, add the mustard powder, Worcestershire sauce, pepper and one tablespoon of the milk. Mix well.

Peel and cut the tomato into thin slices ready for use.

Into a shallow frying pan, put the water and the second tablespoon of milk. Bring to the boil and put in the fillet of haddock and poach in a simmering heat for 3 or 4 minutes on each side. It is cooked when you can loosen the flesh with a fork.

Turn on the grill ready for final cooking.

While poaching the haddock, toast the bread, butter it

and place it in a shallow non-stick metal pan and keep warm.

When the fish is ready, take it out of the frying pan with a fish slice and place it on top of the buttered toast. Then spoon out the cheese mixture and cover the fish thickly. Now put the metal pan under the hot grill and cook until the cheese topping turns golden (about 5 minutes).

Lift the toast with the fish and cheese covering and put it onto the middle of a large dinner plate. Surround it with the thinly sliced tomato.

POACHED SMOKED HADDOCK

Can be served with boiled potatoes and a few rings of cooked carrot.

Preparation time: 5 minutes.   Cooking time: 8–10 minutes.

1 level dessertspn/10g/¼ oz butter
½ cup/90ml milk
1 100g/4 oz fillet of haddock
Seasoning: pepper

Use a 20cm/8″ diameter deep frying pan. Put in the butter, melt it over a low heat and add the milk. Bring to the boil, place in the fillet of smoked haddock and simmer for about 8–10 minutes: allow 2 minutes skin side down, turn onto the flesh side and cook for about 2 minutes, then turn back onto the skin side and cook for 4–6 minutes, depending on the thickness of the fish. Serve on a hot plate and pour over some of the juice. Season with pepper to your liking.

VARIATIONS

If you want to enhance the flavour of this dish, I suggest you add a dessertspoon of Worcestershire sauce to the cooking mixture; or if you like garlic use Chilli and Garlic sauce instead.

When I was about to start cooking this fillet of smoked haddock I remembered I had a decent-sized open mushroom from the day before. Quickly I peeled it, cut it into small pieces, added another knob of butter to the pan and cooked the mushroom pieces at the same time as the fish. It made the dish even tastier and I enjoyed it with 2 small boiled potatoes with the juices from the pan.

KIPPERS

This fish has a high fat content. Kippers vary widely in size: the best are the smaller ones usually available in the summer months.

Cooking only takes about 6 minutes. The best method is to place the kipper in boiling water for 2–3 minutes, drain it and place it under the grill for 3 minutes with a spot of butter on top. In my opinion they are best eaten with slices of brown bread and butter.

If you can buy a large kipper it may be too much for a single meal. What you leave over can be flaked off the skin, kept cool, covered, in the refrigerator and used the next day with eggs, as follows:

NEXT-DAY KIPPER

Preparation time: 4–6 minutes.　Cooking time: 8 minutes.

2 eggs
Pepper (NO salt as the fish is salty enough already)
1 tablespn milk
½ large kipper* (flaked), or some leftovers
1 level dessertspn/10g/¼ oz butter

Beat up the eggs with a fork in a basin. Add some pepper
and the milk, then mix in the flaked kipper.

Melt the butter over a low heat in a medium-sized
saucepan and pour in the mixture. Stir all the time until
the eggs set in a creamy mixture. Serve on hot buttered
toast.

*You can make this dish with flaked smoked haddock. It
will need gentle boiling for 8–10 minutes, depending on
thickness.

MONK FISH AMONTILLADO

This is a fish which you can cut into small scampi-sized
pieces so that when cooked it looks very much like
scampi. This recipe (one of my favourites) is simple to
prepare and if you are unable to buy the monk fish you
can use large-sized prawns instead, although in my
opinion they are not as good.

Serve with new boiled potatoes and a few French beans or
you could eat it with a French baguette available at most
good stores.

Preparation time: 10 minutes.   *Cooking time: 10–12 minutes.*

100g/4 oz monk fish
1 dessertspn cornflour
2 heaped dessertspns/25g/1 oz butter
Seasoning: salt and pepper
1 wine-glass of amontillado sherry
1 tablespn single cream

Cut the monk fish into walnut-sized pieces and coat them with some of the cornflour. You can use any left-over cornflour to thicken the sauce by mixing it with a little water or sherry.

Melt the butter over a medium heat in a deep frying pan, add the monk fish pieces, seasoning, sherry and cream. Heat over a low heat and stir all the time. Ten minutes should be long enough but you do need to reduce the sherry to enhance the flavour. The sauce may need thickening which you can do by stirring in carefully a small amount (maybe a teaspoon) of the cornflour.

The juices in which the fish has been cooked should be poured over the fish when serving.

PAN FRIED PLAICE

This is probably the simplest way to cook a fillet of plaice and very useful if you are in a hurry. It is best eaten with a few new boiled potatoes, cooked with a sprig of mint.

Preparation time: 5 minutes.   *Cooking time: 9 minutes.*

1 heaped dessertspn/15g/½ oz butter
1 dessertspn olive oil
Seasoning: salt and pepper
3 heaped teaspns anchovy purée
125g/5oz fillet of plaice (black skin side as it is usually
thicker)
2 teaspns flour

Melt the butter with the oil in a frying pan over a low heat, adding the salt and pepper to taste, and stir in 1 teaspoon of the anchovy purée. When nicely hot, place in the frying pan the fillet of plaice, flesh side down, and fry for 3 minutes.

Turn the fish with a fish slice onto its black side and cook for a further 6 minutes or until the fish is easy to flake with a fork. During these 6 minutes, baste the flesh with the liquid. You may need to add an extra knob of butter or a splash or two more oil.

Remove the fish to a hot plate and keep it warm.

Mix into the liquid in the pan the remaining anchovy purée and when dissolved, sprinkle in the flour stirring all the time until it thickens. Then pour over the fish and serve.

PLAICE VIN BLANC

You are not likely to see plaice used in *haute cuisine* because it is normally fried in deep fat, or butter, or grilled. It is nevertheless a very pleasing fish. My favourite way of cooking it is as follows which is simple and flavoursome.

A few potatoes can be cooking on the hob with a few young carrots in the same water (or a vegetable of your choice) while the fish is simmering.

Preparation time: 10 minutes.   *Cooking time: 15–20 minutes.*

1 level tablespn/25g/1 oz butter
6 spring onions (chopped and with most of the green parts cut away and discarded)
¾ cup white wine
½ fish stock cube
½ teaspn garlic granules
Seasoning: salt and pepper
1 125g/5 oz fillet of plaice (buy the side with black skin as it is usually thicker)
½ teaspn cornflour

Place the butter into a shallow saucepan or frying pan, add the spring onions, just over half of the white wine, the fish cube dissolved in a small amount of water, garlic and seasoning. Bring to the boil, then simmer for about 3 minutes, stirring to mix well.

Lay in the plaice fillet, flesh side down, and simmer for about 4 minutes, turn over and simmer for another 7 minutes until you can loosen the flesh with a fork.

Remove the fish onto a hot plate and cover. Add the rest of the wine to the pan and reduce the sauce by boiling it for a few minutes, and stirring in the cornflour slowly until the sauce is nicely thickened. Pour over the fish and serve.

SALMON

A superb, versatile fish which today is much lower in price than a good fillet of beef. A tail end steak of salmon can be poached very simply as this recipe shows.

Preparation time: 5 minutes. Cooking time: 10–12 minutes.

1 100g/4 oz salmon steak (about 2cm/¾″ thick)
1 cup (approx.) water
Seasoning: ½ teaspn salt and black pepper
1 teaspn wine vinegar
6 spring onions (finely chopped)

Place the salmon steak into a deep frying pan. Add enough water to come just to the top of the fish, not to cover it. Add the salt and vinegar. Place the onions round the fish and pepper the fish. Bring to the boil and simmer for 10–12 minutes, depending on the thickness of the steak.

LUXURY POACHED SALMON

This is an interesting variation of the previous recipe. It provides a different meal when you wish to entertain a friend: for that you require 2 salmon steaks, but only half as much again of the other ingredients. A few new boiled potatoes, sprinkled with a little chopped parsley, are all you need with this and, perhaps, a glass of the red wine.

Preparation time: 5 minutes.   *Cooking time: about 12 minutes.*

1 level tablespn/25g/1 oz butter
1 fish stock cube dissolved in ½ cup water
½ glass red wine (approx.)
Seasoning: salt and pepper
1 crushed clove of garlic
1 100g/4 oz salmon steak (about 2cm/¾″ thick)

Melt the butter in a frying pan, add the fish stock and wine, salt, pepper and garlic and place the salmon steak into the mixture. Bring to the boil and simmer for 10–12 minutes, turning twice.

Remove the fish onto a pre-heated plate and cover to keep hot or place in the oven on low.

Boil the juices left in the pan to reduce them (which will take a few minutes), then pour over the salmon and serve.

SALMON FISH CAKES

I am very fond of these and they are quite easy to prepare.

Preparation time: 20 minutes.   Cooking time: 26 minutes.

225g/8 oz peeled potatoes
Seasoning: salt and pepper
1 level dessertspn/10g/¼ oz butter
2 teaspns milk (approx.)
1 small (100g/4 oz) tin pink salmon
1 dessertspn finely chopped parsley

Boil the peeled potatoes for about 20 minutes (page 55), drain thoroughly, add the butter and the milk, season and mash well.

Open the tin of salmon into a basin, break it up with a fork, stir in the parsley, then mix it all well into the mashed potatoes.

The mixture then has to be formed into round flat 'burger' shapes. The easy way to do this is to put about a tablespoon of the mixture into an egg ring on a plate, packing it down firmly with the spoon or a fork. Remove the ring and place the shaped mixture into a pan of melted butter and fry until lightly brown on both sides which will take about 3 minutes each side. (If you have no egg ring, you can shape the mixture with floured hands.) They are then ready to serve.

SKATE AU BEURRE

This recipe is one of the most popular ways of serving skate and it is simple to prepare. You need a portion of the wing according to your appetite. A few new potatoes are the only accompaniments you need.

Preparation time: 5 minutes.   *Cooking time: 15 minutes.*

1 skate wing portion (about 100–125g/4–5 oz)
½ teaspn salt
2 teaspn vinegar
Juice of ½ lemon
1 level tablespn/25g/1 oz butter
12 capers
1 dessertspn chopped parsley

The best way to cook skate is to place it in salted, hot water to which you add 1 teaspoon of vinegar and the lemon juice, and then simmer it for 10 minutes. The water should only just cover the fish. Then remove the skate onto a hot plate, cover to keep it hot or place in the oven on low.

While the skate is cooking, start preparing the sauce. Place the butter into a frying pan, add the capers and cook over a low heat until the butter turns a deep brown. Lift the pan off the heat before stirring in the remainder of the vinegar, stir well and pour over the hot fish. Sprinkle over the parsley and serve.

The bones in the skate will be quite soft but will remain crunchy; many people like to eat them.

SOLE MEUNIÈRE

This is one of the simplest ways of cooking fish, although it requires great care. You need to let the butter darken but avoid burning. Depending on the thickness of the fish you may need an extra teaspoon of butter so that there is enough liquid for the cooking. It is very popular in France and is a delicious way to enjoy sole and other white fish. With this, you only need a few new potatoes, boiled with a sprig of mint.

Preparation time: 5 minutes.   *Cooking time: about 8 minutes*

1 heaped dessertspn/15g/½ oz butter
125g/5 oz fillet of sole
Seasoning: salt and pepper
½ teaspn lemon juice (just a squeeze of lemon)

Have a frying pan ready with half the butter in it, and heat. Season the fillet with salt and pepper and place it into the pan when the butter is really hot. Cook it until golden brown on both sides (about 4 minutes each side). Remove the fish onto a hot plate and squeeze a little lemon over it.

Add the rest of the butter to the hot pan and heat the butter until it turns slightly brown, then quickly pour it over the fish and serve.

9

MEAT

In this chapter I include recipes which I have found easy to prepare using beef, lamb, liver, kidneys, pork and sausages. Some of the dishes can be kept in the freezer after cooking and eaten a week or two later.

Beef, one of the most popular meats, is simple to cook. It can be roasted on a spit or in the oven with very little bother. The man alone may not want even a small joint so it is more convenient to buy just sufficient for your immediate needs, say 100–125g (4–5 oz) to grill, fry or braise.

Of course, a small roast joint of beef will provide you with a delicious hot meal and will give you a number of cold slices of meat to eat with salads or in sandwiches; and you can store the joint for a long time in the freezer.

Important: It is essential to keep fresh raw meat in a cold place (such as the refrigerator) and it must not be placed near cooked foods. After purchase, remove the wrapping and keep it on a plate, with another plate upside down on top of it, or keep it in a lidded dish or wrapped tightly in foil.

If you do not want to use it on the same day, you can store it in the freezer for up to 6 months, if correctly wrapped in a plastic airtight box or in a freezer bag. To thaw it, keep it in its packing bag and leave for about 2 hours (for 100g–125g/4–5 oz meat) at kitchen room temperature or leave in the refrigerator for about 5 hours.

Cooked meats (such as casseroles, stews, minced meats and pies, etc.) can be kept in the freezer for 6 months or even longer.

ROAST BEEF

There is nothing nicer than a roasted joint of beef, yet more often than not the only time the man alone can enjoy a few slices of roast beef is at a carvery restaurant or at the home of a friend.

It is however a good idea now and again to buy and cook a small joint for yourself because you can invite one or two friends to enjoy it with you, or you can eat it cold another time.

You need a minimum of 900g (2 lb) of sirloin, ribs or rump and you should ask your butcher for a piece of fat to place on top of the joint to keep the meat moist during cooking.

Potatoes can be roasted in the tin with the meat, but they should be par boiled for 10 minutes before placing round the joint and if medium or large in size they should be cut in half. See page 56. Eat with other vegetables of your choice, such as cauliflower or beans. It is traditional to serve Yorkshire Pudding with the beef (see page 111).

Preparation time: 10 minutes.   Cooking time: 60 minutes. (Cooking time: you need to allow 15 minutes for each 450g/1 lb of beef plus 20 minutes; my timing is for a 900g/ 2 lb joint.)

1 level tablespn/25g/1 oz butter
900g/2 lb joint of beef
1 teaspn gravy browning
½ cup water (preferably used in cooking any vegetables)

Pre-heat the oven on gas 9 (475°F/240°C) and grease a roasting tin with the butter and place in the joint of beef, fat side up. Put the tin into the oven and cook for 20 minutes. Reduce the heat and cook for 30 minutes on gas 4 (350°F/180°C), basting it occasionally.

Take out the joint and place on a hot plate. Gently lift the tin without disturbing the sediment and pour from the corner of the tin the fat floating on the surface into a basin or cup. This will be useful when you need fat for frying. It can be kept in the fridge for up to 4 days. Add the gravy browning to the sediment, then add water from any vegetables you have been cooking, stirring well. This should provide you with plenty of good gravy.

COTTAGE PIE

A great favourite and easy to make.

Preparation time: 10 minutes.   *Cooking time: 25–30 minutes.*

2 potatoes (about 125g/5 oz)
Seasoning: salt and pepper
Few finely chopped mint leaves to taste
1 heaped dessertspn/15g/½ oz butter

(continued overleaf)

(Cottage Pie ingredients, continued)

½ dessertspn milk (or a little more)
1 medium onion (chopped)
100–125g/4–5 oz minced beef
1 small (200g) tin chopped tomatoes
2 small cloves garlic (optional)
1 teaspn cornflour
1 small (150g) tin baked beans
50g/2 oz Cheddar cheese (grated)

Peel the potatoes, cut them into quarters, place them in a small saucepan, cover with water and add half a teaspoon of salt and the chopped mint leaves. Bring to the boil and simmer for about 20 minutes. When you can prick them easily with a fork, they are cooked. They can be simmering while you prepare and cook the meat. When the potatoes are ready, drain away all the water, add the butter, salt and pepper to taste, and the small amount of milk. Mash them well but not too soft, to be ready to spread over the meat.

Put a little oil or meat dripping into a frying pan, add the chopped onion and fry gently until transparent. Add the minced beef and lightly brown all over. Stir to prevent sticking or burning. It should be ready in 10 minutes.

Add the chopped tomatoes and crushed garlic. Mix the cornflour into a little water and add to the meat. Stir and simmer gently for 10 minutes.

To assemble the Cottage Pie, spoon the meat into a small ovenproof dish (about 300ml/½ pint size). Add a layer of heated baked beans. Top with the mashed potato and rake lines across with a fork. Sprinkle with the grated cheese and place under a hot grill for 5 minutes until the cheese browns. It is then ready to serve.

OXTAIL STEW

This is a very enjoyable dish but it does take time to prepare and cook. I advise you to put it in hand the day before you need it and keep it overnight in a cool place (i.e. the refrigerator). This improves its flavour. It will then only need an hour to heat up, although heating for an extra 2 hours makes it even tastier. Serve it with a glass or two of the same wine you use for cooking it.

If you want to entertain, merely include more segments of the oxtail and an extra half cup of red wine.

Ask your butcher to separate the joints of the oxtail and, if possible, purchase three from the base end and one or two from the tail end. You may of course have to buy the whole tail but you can freeze what you do not need and keep for another occasion.

Preparation time: 25 minutes.   *Cooking time: 4 hours or more.*

3-5 oxtail sections, depending on which part of the tail
Flour for sprinkling plus 1 teaspn for thickening
1 medium-sized onion
1 medium-sized carrot
1 large field mushroom
4 stalks celery
2 level dessertspns/15g/½ oz butter
1 dessertspn olive oil
½ cup water
1 dessertspn tomato purée
Seasoning: salt and pepper
1 teaspn garlic granules
1 heaped teaspn paprika
1 cup red wine (preferably Burgundy)

Wash the oxtail joints and dry them on a piece of absorbent kitchen paper. Place them on a large plate and sprinkle over plenty of flour, turning the joints so they are well covered.

Pre-heat the oven on gas 2 (300°F/150°C).

Your main job now is to prepare the vegetables. Peel, slice and chop the onion into small pieces. Clean or scrape the carrot and slice into small rounds. Skin the mushroom, remove its stem and cut into smallish pieces. Wash and chop the celery.

Next, take a deep frying pan, add the butter and oil, heat it and place in the floured pieces of oxtail and fry for 4 or 5 minutes over a moderate heat, turning from time to time until they are nicely browned all over. Remove and place them all into a deep lidded casserole dish.

Mix up the vegetables and pour them all into the casserole dish over the oxtail pieces. (However, if you like your vegetables to remain whole but nicely cooked it is a good idea to retain a third of them and add them about 45 minutes before the end of the 4 hour cooking; or if you prepare and cook the oxtail the day before you wish to eat it, add in the spare third of the vegetables the next day before re-heating for 1 hour in the oven at the same temperature as before.)

Next add the teaspoon of flour into the juices left in the pan in which you browned the oxtail. Sprinkle in the flour, stirring all the time to prevent lumps, and slowly mix in the half cup of water. Bring to the boil and cook for about 1 minute, then pour this sauce into the casserole dish, adding the tomato purée. Add the salt, pepper, garlic granules and paprika and stir well so that the vegetables are well covered. Then pour in the red wine.

Put the lid on the casserole dish and place it into the pre-heated oven and cook for 4 hours (though cooking it for longer than this won't spoil it).

Remove the dish from the oven and, if you don't want to eat it straightaway, keep it in a cool place (e.g. the refrigerator) overnight. If there is a thick skin of fat on the top of it in the morning, scoop it off. The meat should have fallen off the bones so you can remove them and throw them away.

An hour or an hour and a half before you wish to serve the meal, put the casserole dish back into a pre-heated oven (at the same temperature as before). This will give you plenty of time to boil a few new potatoes to enjoy with the stew.

STEAK DIANE

This is a simple dish and a great favourite of mine. You should buy a slice of top quality sirloin or rump steak. Serve on a hot plate with some of the sauce poured over and a few boiled potatoes. This is the correct and best way to serve the dish with no other vegetables required. However, some restaurants will cook Steak Diane with masses of chopped mushrooms and a variety of vegetables.

Preparation time: 6 minutes.   *Cooking time: 8 minutes.*

1 thin slice of steak (100g/4 oz)
1 level tablespn/25g/1 oz butter
8 spring onions/shallots (chopped)
1 dessertspn Worcestershire sauce
1 teaspn chopped fresh parsley or ½ teaspn dried parsley
Seasoning: salt and pepper

First, trim any excess fat or gristle from the meat, then bash it with a rolling pin until it is about 0.5cm/¼″ thick.

In a frying pan melt the butter and in it sauté gently the chopped spring onions (or shallots) until they start to brown. Then place in the steak and sear on both sides. Add the Worcestershire sauce and parsley. You may need another knob or two of butter. Sprinkle the steak with pepper and salt and continue to cook until done to taste (about 4 minutes on each side).

STEAK AND KIDNEY CASSEROLE

This recipe will make 2 or 3 meals when served with boiled potatoes. You can buy the steak and kidneys already prepared in a container at your supermarket.

It is useful because it can be prepared in advance and kept for 3 or 4 days in the cooking pot stored in a cool place (e.g. the refrigerator) or it can be placed in lidded boxes and kept in the freezer for 4 months. Thaw thoroughly before using, then heat well as originally on gas 5 (375°F/190°C) before serving. I like to see it bubble nicely for about 5 minutes. If it is too thick, you can add a little extra wine.

Preparation time: 1½ hours.   *Cooking time: 1½ hours.*

2 teaspns sunflower oil
2 heaped dessertspns/25g/1 oz butter
250g/9 oz steak and kidney
1 medium-sized onion
2 medium-sized mushrooms
2 small carrots
1 small turnip
1 beef stock cube
1 cup water
1 clove crushed garlic
Seasoning: salt and pepper
1½ tablespns flour
1 cup red wine
1 dessertspn tomato purée

Pre-heat the oven on gas 5 (375°F/190°C).

Put the oil and half the butter in a frying pan. When sizzling, add the meat in small pieces in a single layer and brown them to seal the flavour (this takes about 3 minutes). Remove them and put them into a lidded ovenware dish.

Peel and slice the onion, skin the mushrooms and cut into small pieces, scrape the carrots and slice into rounds, add the remainder of the butter and fry all together until the onions are slightly browned. Then put these vegetables into the dish containing the meat. Chop the turnip and add it to the mixture. (If you wish, you could add a sliced-up rasher of bacon to add extra flavour.)

Next mix the beef stock cube in a cup of water and put into the frying pan containing the juices from the vegetables. Add the crushed garlic, salt and pepper, stir in the flour and add the red wine and stir, over a moderate heat, until it thickens (about 5-10 minutes according to taste and whether you prefer it thick or fairly liquid). When ready, pour into the oven-proof dish containing the browned meat, add the tomato purée, stir well, place on the lid and put into the pre-heated oven and cook for 1½ hours. Look at it from time to time: if it is too thick, add a little more water or more wine.

SWEET AND SOUR LAMB CHOPS

This is an easy, tasty and quick way to cook one or two lamb chops and makes a welcome change from the usual custom of serving with mint.

Preparation time: 5 minutes plus ½–1 hour marinating.
Cooking time: 16–20 minutes.

1 level dessertspn/10g/¼ oz butter
1 or 2 lamb chops (2.75cm/1¼" thick, 115g/4½ oz approx.)
Seasoning: salt and pepper
2 teaspns Chilli and Garlic sauce per chop
2 teaspns Seville orange marmalade per chop

In a small grill pan melt the butter. Score the chop(s) deeply on both sides with a sharp knife and place them on the buttered pan. Season well with salt and pepper. Then pour on a teaspoon of the Chilli and Garlic sauce and let it seep into the cuts for a few seconds, turn it over and put a teaspoon of the same on the other side. Leave them to marinate for 30 minutes to 1 hour. During this time you can prepare ready for cooking whatever vegetables you like.

Turn on the grill. Spread a teaspoon of marmalade on each side of each chop, place under the grill and cook for 8 minutes until sizzling and lightly brown. Then, turn and cook the other side for 6 minutes. Meanwhile, cook your potatoes and/or other vegetables.

Remove the cooking pan and take out the cooked chop(s) and place on a hot plate. Take 2 or 3 teaspoons of the juices and pour over the chop(s), add the vegetables and you are ready to enjoy a delightful meal.

GRILLED LAMB CHOPS

For a substantial meal, buy yourself a double chop; some butchers call this a butterfly or Barnsley chop. Each chop should be about 2cm/¾" thick. They reduce slightly during cooking. For a smaller meal, just buy a single good-sized chop. If you want less fat, the butcher will cut it off for you.

Serve with boiled potatoes and French beans which can be cooking at the same time. Both the vegetables will cook nicely in the same water and will only take about 20 minutes.

Preparation time: 8 minutes.   *Cooking time: 25 minutes.*

1 teaspn sunflower oil
1 lamb chop
Seasoning: black pepper, dried rosemary
½ chicken stock cube
1 cup water
½ teaspn gravy browning
1 heaped teaspn tomato purée
1 pinch garlic granules

Brush the oil on both sides of the chop and place it in a shallow non-stick cooking tin. Sprinkle the black pepper and rosemary on and around the chop. Put the tin under a hot grill (using the second shelf down if possible) and cook for 10 minutes on each side.

While cooking, mix the half stock cube in the water, then mix in the gravy browning, tomato purée and the garlic. Pour into a small saucepan and bring to the boil. When the meat is cooked, pour the juices from the cooking tin into the sauce mixture. When the sauce is nicely thickened (about 5–10 minutes according to taste and whether you prefer it thick or fairly liquid), it should be poured round the chop and served on a hot plate.

LIVER AND BACON

You can use lamb's liver but calf's liver is best and, of course, more costly. I prefer to use best back bacon and so often use a knob of butter when frying. Streaky bacon will give the most fat.

Eat with a French crispy roll or bread and butter.

Preparation time: 5 minutes.   Cooking time: 8–10 minutes.

75g/3 oz liver (cut into 3 slices)
1 dessertspn flour seasoned with salt and pepper
2 bacon rashers
1 teaspn cornflour
¼ cup water
1 teaspn Worcestershire sauce

Sprinkle the slices of liver with the seasoned flour, then shake off any surplus.

Fry the rashers of bacon. When almost cooked, push the bacon to one side and add the slices of liver to the pan. Cook each side of the liver for 3–4 minutes but make sure you don't overcook it: it should be served quite pink. Finish off cooking the bacon to your liking.

When ready, put the liver and bacon onto a hot plate and keep hot while you make the gravy. Mix the cornflour into the water with the Worcestershire sauce and boil this in the pan with the juices from the liver until it thickens. Pour over the bacon and liver and serve.

TASTY KIDNEYS

This is a simple and enjoyable way to cook kidneys. A few cooked noodles go well with them (page 69).

Preparation time: 10 minutes.   Cooking time: 8 minutes.

3 lamb's kidneys
Seasoning: salt and pepper
2 medium-sized mushrooms
1 heaped dessertspn/15g/½ oz butter
1 dessertspn olive oil
1 teaspn mustard powder
1 teaspn curry powder
1 dessertspn milk

Skin, core and quarter the kidneys, season them with salt and pepper. Remove the stems from the mushrooms, then skin them and cut into small pieces.

Melt the butter in the frying pan over a moderate heat, adding the olive oil and heat. Add the kidneys and mushrooms. Fry for 4 minutes. While you are doing this, mix the mustard and the curry powder with the milk, pour this into the frying pan and cook for 4 minutes more on a simmering heat. If you want the sauce to be thicker, add a dessertspoon of cream, stirring it in well.

SAVOURY PORK

You will need a few boiled potatoes to go with this dish.
You can buy sour cream at superstores, but you can also
make it by squeezing some lemon juice into ordinary
cream.

Preparation time: 10 minutes.   Cooking time: 40 minutes.

2 heaped dessertspns/25g/1 oz butter
½ medium-sized onion
1 dessertspn/15g/½ oz flour
Seasoning: salt and pepper
1 pork fillet (115g/4½ oz approx.)
1 teaspn paprika
¼ teaspn cayenne pepper
1 cooking apple
1 tablespn water
½ cup sour cream

Melt the butter in a lidded saucepan over a medium heat.
Peel, slice and chop the onion and add it to the pan. Cook
on a medium heat for about 5 minutes until soft and
slightly brown.

Season the flour with salt and pepper and coat the fillet of
pork in it. Push the onion to one side of the saucepan and
place the meat into the pan, then brown it slightly on both
sides (about 5 minutes). Then add the paprika and
cayenne. Put the lid on the saucepan and simmer on a
very low heat for 30 minutes until the meat is tender,
turning it 2 or 3 times.

While the main dish is cooking, peel, core and chop the
apple. Put it into another small saucepan with the water,
bring to the boil, then simmer for about 10 minutes until

nicely cooked. Time this so that the apple sauce is ready at the same time as the pork.

Two minutes before serving, pour the sour cream into the saucepan containing the meat and stir well. You are then ready to serve the savoury pork with the apple sauce nicely warm alongside.

TASTY GAMMON STEAK

For this recipe you should use fresh (not dried) bread-crumbs so you need to crumble a slice from a large loaf with the crust removed, or (if you have a food processor) you only need a slice from a small loaf, including the crust.

A few hot peas will go well with this dish, together with boiled potatoes or just bread and butter, plus a cup of strong coffee.

Preparation time: 10–15 minutes.   Cooking time:16–18 minutes.

1 dessertspn/25g/1 oz grated Gruyère or Parmesan cheese
1 dessertspn fresh breadcrumbs
1 teaspn mustard powder
1 teaspn garlic granules
100g/4 oz gammon (about 1cm/½" thick)

Mix the cheese with the breadcrumbs and add the mustard powder and garlic granules.

Heat the grill. Place the gammon onto a baking dish and put it under the grill (one shelf down if possible) and cook for 7 minutes. Turn it over and grill the other side for another 5 minutes.

Remove the gammon from the heat and spread the cheese mixture over it, return it to the grill and cook until it is crisp and slightly brown (about 4 or 5 minutes).

SAUSAGES

There is a large variety of sausages available in shops today. There are thick and thin sausages and chipolatas, as well as sausages with various flavours. Some are made from pork, some from beef and some from a mixture of meats. You will find Dorset, Lincolnshire, French style and Cumberland (which are made in considerable length) sausages all on sale.

German spiced sausages can be used if preferred in all my sausage recipes, unless stated otherwise.

FRIED SAUSAGES

Serve on a hot plate with mashed potatoes (see page 56).

Preparation time: 5 minutes.   Cooking time: 20 minutes.

2 or 3 pork sausages
1 level dessertspn/10g/¼ oz butter
1 teaspn cooking oil
1 large French tomato (or 3 small ordinary ones)

Prick the sausages with a fork in a few places to prevent them bursting. Take a medium-sized frying pan and put in the butter and oil, heat gently on medium and place in the sausages. Simmer for about 20 minutes, turning regularly to brown them all over.

Cut the large tomato into 4 sections (cut small ones in halves). After the sausages have been cooking for about 12 minutes, drop the tomatoes into the frying pan, and they will be ready by the time the sausages are cooked.

I like to eat this with a half slice of white bread which is fried in the juices left in the pan after the sausages and tomatoes have been removed; but you may need another knob or two of butter to fry this.

OVEN BAKED SAUSAGES

This is an easy and delightful way to enjoy sausages, especially if the sausages have been made with some garlic. With this method, there's no spluttering over the hob which occurs when you fry them.

Preparation time: 3 minutes.   *Cooking time: 24 minutes.*

2 teaspns olive oil
2 or 3 sausages

Pre-heat the oven on gas 3 (325°F/170°C).

Smear the bottom and sides of a shallow non-stick metal tin with the olive oil (I use a finger for this), then add the sausages. Place the tin in the oven on one shelf from the top. Cook for 20 minutes, turning the sausages occasionally. Take out the tin and place it under a hot grill for 4 minutes, turning the sausages once to make them nicely brown all over. They are then ready.

While the sausages are in the oven, you can cook some potatoes and French beans to enjoy with them. Cook the potatoes as per page 55. After 10 minutes, put the French beans (straight from the refrigerator or freezer) into the boiling water with the potatoes; they only take 10 minutes to cook.

Strain off the water from the vegetables, remove the beans to a hot plate, add a teaspoon of milk and a level dessertspoon/10g/¼ oz of butter (or a little more if you like them more creamy), salt and pepper and mash the potatoes well. Then serve alongside the sausages.

POACHED SAUSAGES

Another handy way to cook sausages is to poach them. With this method there is no spitting, as occurs when frying them in fat, so you don't have to clean the hob afterwards. Serve with mashed potatoes.

Why not poach 4 or 6 sausages and keep the extra ones to eat cold another day? For this you may need a drop more milk and butter.

Preparation time: 8 minutes.   *Cooking time: 25 minutes.*

1 small onion (well chopped)
1 cup/150ml/¼ pint milk
Seasoning: salt and pepper
2 or 3 pork sausages
½ teaspn gravy browning
1 dessertspn water
1 heaped dessertspn/15g/½ oz butter

Put the onion and the milk into a frying pan, season to taste, heat gently and add the sausages. Turn the heat up and cook for 25 minutes, turning the sausages from time to time to make them nicely brown all over.

While the sausages are poaching, mix the gravy browning into a paste with the water.

Remove the sausages to a hot plate and cover them to keep them warm.

Add the gravy paste with the butter to the onion mixture in the frying pan. Mix well, bring to the boil and cook for about 3 minutes until nicely thick. Then pour over the sausages and serve.

SAUSAGE YORKSHIRE PUDDING

A useful and filling dish which is quite simple to make. It is often referred to as 'Toad-in-the-Hole'. Potatoes and broccoli or peas go well with it.

Preparation time: 10 minutes.   Cooking time: 30 minutes.

4 dessertspns/50g/2 oz plain flour
⅔ cup/150ml/¼ pint milk
Seasoning: salt, cayenne pepper, dried thyme
1 egg
2 or 3 pork sausages
1 level dessertspn/10g/¼ oz butter
1 tablespn water

Pre-heat the oven on gas 7 (425°F/220°C).

Prepare the batter. Put the flour into a basin, add the milk gradually and mix into a paste, seasoning with a pinch of salt and a good sprinkling of cayenne pepper and thyme. Beat the egg in a cup with a fork and pour into the flour mix and stir well into a creamy mixture.

Prick the sausages several times with a fork to prevent them bursting and place them in a frying pan with a knob of the butter and cook over a moderate heat, turning them over until they are slightly brown all over. Take them out and put them, side by side but not touching each other, into a metal dish greased on the bottom and sides with a knob of butter. The dish should be about 5cm/2″ deep and 12.5cm–15cm/5–6″ diameter (either square or round).

Pour the batter over the sausages and put the dish into the preheated oven and cook for 25–30 minutes. Remove it when it has risen and is nicely brown on the highest parts, mainly round the sides. Serve on a hot plate heated on top of or inside the oven.

PLAIN YORKSHIRE PUDDING

Make the batter as opposite. Grease an oven-proof dish (or a tray with individual bun compartments) and pour in the batter. Then cook as above.

10

CHICKEN

Chicken can be cooked and served in a variety of ways with a wide selection of sauces. It is available in pre-cooked and also pre-packed form at most supermarkets and shops.

OVEN BOILED (POT ROAST) CHICKEN

This is my favourite way of cooking a chicken because you retain all the flavour and you are left with very useful stock which makes a good base for soup and which you can freeze and keep for another time.

Buy a ready-to-cook prepared chicken for this. Serve slices of the breast with croquette potatoes (see page 57) or just ordinary boiled potatoes, French beans, sliced courgettes or carrots.

Preparation time: 10 minutes.　　　*Cooking time: 2 hours.*

1 chicken (1.1kg/2½ lb)
1 chopped onion (100g/4 oz)
1 garlic clove (chopped) or ½ teaspn garlic powder
1 bouquet garni (on sale in small bags; remember to remove after cooking)

Seasoning: salt and pepper
825ml/1½ pints (approx.) water

Pre-heat the oven on gas 7 (425°F/220°C).

Place the chicken in a fairly large oven-proof pot, deep enough to allow a reasonable space all round. Surround the chicken with the onion and garlic. Add the bouquet garni and the salt and pepper. Fill the pot with water to just over half way up the bird. Place in the oven and cook for 2 hours.

When the chicken is cold you can eat the rest of the cold breast with a salad a day or two later. The remainder of the meat should be cut off, its legs and wings removed and placed in mealsized portions in freezer bags and kept in the freezer for the future, perhaps for using in Chicken Madras (page 119).

To make chicken stock, pour off the excess juices from the boiled chicken into a basin. When cold, transfer into a few small containers and put in the freezer. It will be useful from time to time when you want to make sauces.

CHICKEN FINE HERBS

Serve with French beans and potatoes and perhaps a glass of white wine.

Preparation time: 8 minutes.   Cooking time: 15 minutes.

1 heaped dessertspn/15g/½ oz butter
1 chicken breast
1 tablespn flour
½ teaspn thyme
½ teaspn sage
½ teaspn rosemary
½ teaspn cardamom
½ teaspn tarragon
⅓ cup white wine

Melt the butter in a frying pan over a moderate heat.

Slice the breast of the chicken into 5 or 6 strips, depending on the thickness of the breast. Sprinkle them with the flour and place them in the butter and cook until tender (about 15 minutes), turning them 2 or 3 times during cooking. After cooking for about 5 minutes sprinkle over the herbs and spices. Make sure the meat is white inside each slice (i.e. well cooked) by testing with a fork.

Remove the chicken onto a hot plate, then add the white wine to the juices in the frying pan, simmer until this sauce thickens a little and pour it over the chicken.

SPICY TOMATO CHICKEN

Enjoy with vegetables of your choice. Boiled potatoes can be cooking while you follow this recipe. If you only eat half this dish, you can put the rest into a plastic box when cold and freeze for future use for up to 6 months.

Preparation time: 20 minutes.   *Cooking time: 30 minutes.*

1 small onion
2 teaspns butter
1 dessertspn sunflower oil
1 tablespn flour
Seasoning: salt and pepper
1 chicken portion (breast or leg)
1 teaspn curry powder (or more if you like it really hot)
1 teaspn mixed herbs
1 small (225g/8 oz) tin tomatoes
1 tablespn/15g/½ oz sultanas
1 tablespn/15g/½ oz split almonds
½ teaspn nutmeg

Peel, cut and chop the onion quite finely.

In a shallow saucepan (which has a lid) melt the butter and oil over a medium heat. Season the flour, push the chicken portion through it until it is nicely covered all over, then place it in the pan over a moderate heat and fry for about 5 minutes until it is a golden brown. Add the onion, curry powder, mixed herbs and remaining flour, stir well and fry for another 3 minutes.

Remove the saucepan from the heat, push the chicken to one side, add the tomatoes, sultanas and almonds, stirring well. Add the nutmeg.

Now move the chicken into the centre of the pan, cover it with the moist tomato mixture, put on the saucepan lid and simmer for 20 minutes until the chicken is nicely tender. Look at it from time to time to make sure the moisture has not dried out. It should be quite thick but you do not want it to burn. Add a spoonful of water if necessary.

CHICKEN BREAST WITH MUSHROOMS

With this you only need a few new potatoes.

Preparation time: 15 minutes.   *Cooking time: 15–20 minutes.*

2 medium-sized mushrooms
1 heaped dessertspn/15g/½ oz butter
1 chicken breast
1 level dessertspn plain flour
½ chicken stock cube
½ cup white wine or water
½ teaspn cinnamon
2 cloves
1 tablespn cream

First, skin and chop the mushrooms, discarding the stalks, so they are ready when required towards the end of cooking.

Melt the butter in a pan on a medium heat and place in the chicken breast. Fry for 10 minutes, turning 2 or 3 times, and remove onto a hot plate.

Sprinkle the flour into the hot butter in the pan, mix and heat until it browns slightly. Dissolve the half stock cube in the wine (not essential, you can dissolve it in water) and pour it into the flour-butter mix, stirring well.

Add the mushrooms and cook for 5 minutes. Add the cinnamon, the cloves and cream. Stir well and pour over the chicken.

CHICKEN SUPREME

This is one of the simplest ways of cooking breast of chicken which you can buy in a packet from your local superstore or butcher. Serve with potatoes or boiled rice.

Preparation time: 5 minutes.   *Cooking time: 10 minutes.*

1 chicken breast
1 heaped dessertspn/15g/½ oz butter
Seasoning: salt and pepper
1 teaspn lemon juice
A sprinkle of nutmeg

Pre-heat the oven on gas 8 (450°F/230°C).

All you have to do is to cut the breast of the chicken into 3 slices with a sharp knife, smooth them over with melted butter, salt and pepper them well, then place them into a well buttered oven-proof lidded baking dish. Sprinkle over the lemon juice, then place the dish (with the lid on) into the pre-heated oven and cook for 10 minutes when the meat should be nicely tender but not over-browned. Dust over a little nutmeg.

VARIATION
Lay the cooked chicken breast on a bed of boiled spinach (which takes about 8 minutes to cook, see page 65) and then cover the chicken with 2 or 3 tablespoons of Mornay Sauce (see page 130), sprinkle with a little grated cheese and put under a hot grill for 3–5 minutes so that it browns slightly.

CHICKEN MADRAS

This is a simple way to use one of the chicken legs you removed from your boiled chicken (page 112) and kept in the freezer or a pre-cooked chicken leg bought from your local superstore. Make sure that any frozen chicken is thoroughly defrosted before use; this can take 5–6 hours.

Preparation time: 15–20 minutes.   *Cooking time: 25 minutes.*

1 cooked chicken leg
2 heaped dessertspns/25g/1 oz butter
6 spring onions (or ½ small onion)
1 dessertspn sultanas
1 teaspn lemon juice
1 dessertspn chutney (I recommend fruit and nut chutney or mango chutney)
½ chicken stock cube
300ml/½ pint water
Black pepper
1½ teaspns Madras curry powder
1 teaspn gravy browning
2 dessertspns rice

Take the flesh off the chicken leg, cut it into bite-sized pieces. Melt the butter gently in a lidded saucepan and add the chicken to it.

Clean the spring onions, remove their excess green leaves and chop the remainder into small pieces. Add to the chicken in the saucepan, along with the sultanas, lemon juice, chutney and the chicken stock cube dissolved in the water (you may have chicken stock in your freezer which you can use instead of the stock cube). Sprinkle with the black pepper and the curry powder. Stir and bring the contents to the boil and simmer for 20–25 minutes.

Mix the gravy browning in a tablespoon of water and pour into the saucepan after 10 minutes of the simmering and complete the cooking.

While cooking the chicken you can prepare the rice. It is easiest to buy a tin of pre-cooked long grain rice which only needs 3 minutes to heat (follow the instructions on the tin). Or you can use a single portion from a carton of long grain rice which will take 20 minutes to cook. Or see page 66.

CHICKEN WINE CASSEROLE

This recipe makes use of left-overs from a cooked chicken. You can use a bought uncooked portion instead, but this will need an extra 5–10 minutes cooking.

Serve with boiled potatoes. These will take about 20 minutes (see page 55) and can be cooked at the same time as the casserole. You can also serve the casserole with croûtons (see page 135).

Preparation time: 20–25 minutes.   *Cooking time: 30 minutes.*

1 cooked chicken leg
1 medium-sized (40g/2½ oz approx.) tomato
1 bunch spring onions
1 medium-sized open mushroom
2 heaped dessertspns/25g/1 oz butter
1 dessertspn olive oil
1 level teaspn bouquet garni (or if you use a bag of bouquet

garni, remember to remove the bag when cooked)
Seasoning: salt and pepper
2 teaspns Chilli and Garlic sauce
1 wine-glass red wine (I prefer Beaujolais)
½ teaspn gravy browning

Take the chicken meat off the bone and cut into moderate-sized pieces. Peel the tomato (the skin comes off easily if you place it in hot water for a minute) and slice into quarters. Remove and discard excess green leaves from the spring onions and chop them finely. Skin and cut the mushroom into small pieces.

Take a shallow saucepan with a lid, put in the butter and oil and melt over a medium heat. Add the onions and mushroom and fry for a few minutes until soft, move to one side and add the chicken. Fry it until slightly brown (about 5 minutes).

Add the tomato sections, stir together, scatter over the bouquet garni, seasoning and Chilli and Garlic sauce, pour in the red wine, bring to the boil, then simmer for up to 25 minutes with the lid on.

Mix the gravy browning in a cup with a dessertspoon of water and pour into the saucepan about 10 minutes before it is ready to serve. This will thicken the sauce.

11

VEGETARIAN DISHES

Nuts, pulses, grains and pastas, in addition to vegetables, form the basis of a vegetarian diet and all are readily available in supermarkets and health food shops. It is always useful to have a selection of these in your store cupboard, along with spices and herbs. Being versatile, they can be turned quickly into a tasty dish when added to a vegetable casserole or simply cooked slowly with various spices and herbs. They add both texture and body, as well as being extremely nourishing.

One of the beauties of vegetarian cookery is that the variations on any theme seem to be endless. The few recipes included here are useful and handy examples, so do not hesitate to experiment.

A vegetable stock is needed for many dishes, and stock cubes can be bought from shops.

MUSHROOM CRUMBLE

A glass of red wine, such as Fleurie, makes a nice accompaniment.

Preparation time: 10 minutes.   *Cooking time: 12–14 minutes.*

3 tablespns breadcrumbs
4 tablespns grated mature Cheddar cheese
1 level dessertspn/10g/¼ oz butter
½ small onion (finely chopped)
75g/3 oz field mushrooms (finely chopped)
1 teaspn mixed herbs
Seasoning: salt and pepper

Mix the breadcrumbs and cheese thoroughly and put to one side.

Melt the butter over a medium heat in a non-stick frying pan and when it starts to foam add the onion and cook until transparent (about 3 minutes). Then add the mushrooms, herbs and seasoning and cook gently, shaking the pan frequently, for 3–4 minutes until the mushrooms are soft.

Take a deep oven-proof dish or tin about 10cm/4″ in diameter, grease with butter and pack in the onion and mushrooms, then cover with the breadcrumb and cheese mixture. Now place the dish/tin under a hot grill and leave it for about 4 minutes until the top is golden brown.

You can serve from the dish in which it has been cooked or scoop it out onto a hot plate or onto a slice of hot buttered toast.

BUTTER BEANS AU GRATIN

A simple recipe for a tasty, hot dish.

Preparation time: 20 minutes approx.   Cooking time: 15–20 minutes.

100g/4 oz butter beans (½ small 220g/8 oz tin)
150ml/¼ pint white sauce (see page 129)
2 tablespns grated Parmesan or Cheddar cheese
Seasoning: salt and pepper
1 level dessertspn/10g/¼ oz butter
2 level tablespns/25g/1 oz breadcrumbs

Pre-heat the oven on gas 4 (350°F/180°C), if using.

Put the butter beans into a large saucepan with water to cover (do **not** use the liquid from the tin) and heat on a moderate heat for about 5 minutes until they are nicely hot.

In another saucepan make the white sauce, adding two-thirds of the cheese and the seasoning. Pour this over the beans, stir and warm thoroughly.

Grease a small oven-proof dish and pour the mixture in, then sprinkle over the breadcrumbs and dot with knobs of butter on top. Place in the pre-heated oven for about 10 minutes, or under a hot grill for 5–7 minutes, until the breadcrumbs are lightly browned.

NUT ROAST

You will need a food processor for this recipe.

Preparation time: 15 minutes.   Cooking time: 40 minutes.

½ large (115g/4 oz) onion
1 tablespn/25g/1 oz polyunsaturated margarine
100g/4 oz mixed nuts (peanuts, walnuts, cashews, hazel-
    nuts, or your own choice)
1 cup/50g/2 oz wholemeal breadcrumbs
1 teaspn mixed herbs
1 teaspn garlic granules (or 2 crushed cloves)
1 teaspn yeast extract (mixed in ⅓ cup water)
1 tomato

Pre-heat the oven on gas 4 (350°F/150°C).

Peel, cut and finely chop the onion. Cook it in some of the
margarine in a frying pan over a medium heat for about 4
minutes until soft but not browned, then put it into a
basin.

Grind the nuts in a food processor and place with the
onion. Add 2 tablespoons of the breadcrumbs, the herbs,
garlic and the yeast extract mixed in the water. Mix well
with a fork.

Peel and slice the tomato and place in the bottom of a
shallow oven-proof dish, then scoop the nut mix on top of
it, smoothing it level. Next sprinkle the remainder of the
breadcrumbs over the top. Place into the pre-heated oven
and cook for 30 minutes.

COURGETTE PROVENÇALE

This is really quite delicious and can be used as a starter or as a snack. One advantage is you can prepare and cook it in your spare time and eat it cold later. However, I like it hot.

Preparation time: 15 minutes.   Cooking time: 25 minutes.

½ **medium-sized onion**
1 **medium-sized tomato**
2 **medium-sized courgettes**
2 **tablespns olive oil**
1 **teaspn garlic granules**
Seasoning: salt and pepper
½ **teaspn thyme**
½ **cup water**
1 **tablespn chopped parsley**

Peel, slice and chop the onion. Peel and chop the tomato. Slice the courgettes into rings about 5mm/¼″ thick. Heat the olive oil in a pan with a lid. When the oil is nicely hot, add the courgette rings and fry for about 10 minutes, turning the slices over to brown them slightly on both sides.

Remove the courgettes, then add the onion to the pan with the garlic granules and fry until the onion pieces are soft (about 3 minutes). Push them to one side and add the tomato. Sprinkle with the salt, pepper and thyme, then continue cooking for a further 3 minutes.

Return the courgettes to the pan with the other vegetables, add the water and bring to the boil, then simmer with the lid on for about 6 minutes. If the mixture is too liquid, bring to the boil again for a short time to reduce

the liquid, although this is not normally necessary.
Sprinkle the parsley over before serving.

LEEK LOAF

This recipe makes enough for 2 servings and as it can also
be enjoyed cold you can keep half in the refrigerator to
eat another day. I like to eat it with the Greek yoghurt
sauce detailed below and a slice of bread and butter.

Preparation time: 20 minutes.   Cooking time: 45 minutes.

1 egg
2 medium-sized leeks
1 medium-sized carrot
2 dessertspns olive oil
1 cup/50g/2 oz dried breadcrumbs
1 tablespn fresh parsley (chopped)
1 tablespn chives/spring onions (chopped)
3 dessertspns sunflower seeds
Seasoning: salt and pepper

Pre-heat the oven on gas 4 (350°F/180°C).

Crack the egg into a basin and beat it. Wash the leeks
thoroughly. Slice and chop the white parts and most of the
green parts of the leeks. Clean and grate the carrot fairly
fine. Add the oil and stir well. Put it all into a non-stick
frying pan and fry for 5 or 6 minutes until the vegetables
are softened, then add the breadcrumbs a little at a time,
the parsley and the chives/spring onions, sunflower seeds
and seasoning, turning the mixture regularly with a non-
stick fish slice. Let it cool slightly before adding the
beaten egg and stirring again.

Now press the mixture down tightly into a greased (with butter) non-stick baking tin and cover the top with foil. Place into the pre-heated oven and bake for 40 minutes.

When cooked, knife round the sides to loosen it slightly, turn the tin upside-down onto a hot plate or dish and the loaf should come out onto the plate ready to cut and eat.

This loaf can be served with the following tasty thick sauce:

1 dessertspn Greek yoghurt
1 teaspn mayonnaise
1 splash lemon juice
1 teaspn parsley (finely chopped)

Mix all the ingredients together and serve either over or alongside the loaf. (This sauce is also good with poached white fish.)

12

SAUCES

A good sauce can enliven a simple dish but it does take time to prepare.

WHITE BUTTER (BEURRE BLANC) SAUCE

This sauce is the basis for many others. It can be made 2 or 3 days in advance and kept in the refrigerator. Alternatively, it can be frozen in quarter or half pint quantities which you can thaw out by stirring over a gentle heat when required.

Preparation time: 3–5 minutes. Cooking time: 3–5 minutes.

1 heaped dessertspn/15g/½ oz butter
1 dessertspn cornflour (or ordinary flour)
Seasoning: salt and pepper to taste
1 cup milk

Melt the butter in a small saucepan over a medium heat. Add the flour gradually, mixing it well, then sprinkle in the salt and pepper. Pour in the milk slowly and beat it thoroughly over a low heat until nicely creamy (about 3–5 minutes). If it becomes too thick, add a little more milk until it is sufficiently runny for the dish you are serving it with.

VARIATIONS

You can add to the basic white sauce a beef-, fish- or chicken-flavoured stock cube well mixed in half a cup of water. You can also add a beaten egg yolk but make sure you merely warm the sauce when adding the egg and don't boil it.

If you become an enthusiastic cook, you can experiment by adding other things to your white sauce, such as capers and a little lemon juice, or a half cup of white wine.

MORNAY SAUCE

This sauce is used extensively with fish, particularly with cod, plaice and even with salmon.

Prepare the basic white butter sauce as above, adding a dessertspoon of grated Parmesan cheese (or hard mature Cheddar) and half a teaspoon of mustard powder to the mixture and stirring well over a low heat.

MUSTARD SAUCE

This is a popular sauce to serve with herrings and other fish. It is also served with various meat dishes.

Prepare the basic white butter sauce as above, adding a teaspoon of English mustard powder and half a teaspoon of French mustard.

ONION SAUCE

This sauce goes well with chicken and lamb.

Preparation time: 8 minutes.   *Cooking time: about 25 minutes.*

1 medium-sized 75g/3 oz onion
1 stick of celery (optional)
Seasoning: salt and pepper
Quantity of white butter sauce (see page 129)
1 dessertspn Chilli and Garlic sauce
2 tablespns cream

Peel, slice and chop the onion into smallish pieces, cut the celery into 0.5cm/¼″ pieces and place the onion and celery into a saucepan of water, add the seasoning, cover and boil until tender (about 20 minutes). Drain well, add to the white butter sauce with the Chilli and Garlic sauce, mix well, simmer for 5 minutes, add the cream and it is ready to serve.

BÉCHAMEL SAUCE

This is a basic and important sauce to which you can add various items to suit your cooking, such as mushrooms, parsley, cheese, wine, etc. When you become really interested in cooking, this sauce can be developed to add extra and special flavours to many dishes.

Preparation time: 8 minutes.   *Cooking time: 25 minutes.*

1 cup milk
4 spring onions or ½ 100g/4 oz onion (finely chopped)
2 cloves
Seasoning: salt and pepper
¼ teaspn ground nutmeg
1 heaped dessertspn/15g/½ oz butter
1 dessertspn cornflour (or ordinary flour)
½ cup water

Pour the milk into a small saucepan, adding the finely chopped onions, cloves, seasoning and nutmeg, stir and bring to the boil, then gently simmer for 20 minutes.

Melt the butter over a low heat, mixing in the flour, adding a little water and stirring it into a thick cream while continuing to heat. Strain the milk (thereby removing the cooked onion) into the butter and flour. Bring it back to the boil for a minute or two, stirring well.

You can use this as a thickish sauce or can dilute it with a drop or two of milk or water or a splash or two of white wine to your liking.

APPLE SAUCE

Serve warm with pork and other meats to your liking.

Preparation time: 8 minutes.   Cooking time: 10 minutes.

1 or 2 cooking apples
1 or 2 tablespns water
1 or 2 teaspns caster sugar
1 teaspn cinnamon (or squeeze of ½ a lemon)

According to the amount of sauce you require, peel, core and cut 1 or 2 apples into small pieces. Simmer them in a small saucepan with about a tablespoon of water per apple until nicely soft (about 10 minutes), stirring to prevent burning.

When cooked, mash the apples well or mix them in a food processor, adding a teaspoon of sugar per apple and the cinnamon or lemon juice.

SHERRY SAUCE

Serve this sauce hot. It is particularly suitable for shellfish.

Preparation time: 3 or 4 minutes. Cooking time: 2 minutes.

1 level tablespn/25g/1 oz butter
⅓ cup sherry (amontillado)
½ cup thick cream
Sprinkle of salt
½ teaspn paprika

Melt the butter in a small saucepan over a medium heat, add the sherry and simmer for 2 minutes, adding the cream, seasoning with salt and paprika and stirring well.

READY-MADE SAUCES

There is a large selection of sauces available in most superstores and small shops. It is advisable to keep a selection in your kitchen as they add an appetising flavour to many simple dishes and are time-saving too. Here are a few that I find useful.

CHILLI AND GARLIC
Can be used to add a gently garlic flavour with its spicy blend of chilli and other ingredients.

GINGER AND ORANGE
Is particularly good with salads, duck, turkey and shellfish such as prawns. It is a mellow blend of citrus, ginger, sherry and aromatic spices.

HOT PEPPER AND LIME
Has a refreshing tangy flavour of lime with hot pepper which can be used with pork, lamb and other meats.

SOY
Is used mainly in Chinese dishes and many rice recipes. It is made from the Far Eastern soy bean and is slightly sweet.

WORCESTERSHIRE
Is particularly useful and can add a distinctive flavour to meats, stews, casseroles and a variety of fish dishes.

CROÛTES AND CROÛTONS

Croûtons are small pieces of fried bread which are simple to make. They are served with soups or as a garnish for stews and casseroles and are normally made in small 1cm/½" squares. However, I like to prepare fairly large size croûtons (croûtes) which I use as a starter when entertaining.

Preparation time: 8–10 minutes.   *Cooking time: about 6 minutes.*

2 or more white bread slices (preferably slightly stale)
2 level dessertspns/15g/½ oz butter
1 dessertspn olive oil
Seasoning: a sprinkle of salt and pepper
1 teaspn garlic granules

Cut 2 slices (about 1cm/½" thick) from a large white loaf. Remove the crusts, then cut out 2 circles from each slice (with a diameter of about 5cm/2"). A good way to do this is to take a wine glass and press it into the soft centre of each slice so that it marks out a clean circle which you can cut out with a pair of kitchen scissors.

Next put the butter and olive oil into a non-stick frying pan and heat. Add a pinch of salt and pepper and the garlic granules and stir. Place the rounds of bread into the pan and fry each side until golden brown. The bread will absorb the liquid and you may have to add an extra knob of butter. The amount of butter and oil needed will depend on the number of rounds. Browning will take about 2 or 3 minutes each side.

Remove the circles of bread when browned and drain them on some absorbent kitchen paper. They are ready to eat hot, but when cold can be kept in the refrigerator or put into polythene bags and kept for up to 4 weeks in the freezer. You can thaw them in a hot oven in about 5 minutes.

VARIATIONS
Your guest(s) will certainly be impressed with your chef's skills if you serve them any of the following!

Make 4 round croûtes and spread over the top of each a 0.5cm/¼″ slice of Italian Gorgonzola cheese and place under a hot grill for about 3 minutes until it begins to melt and brown.

Make a small amount of white butter sauce (page 129). Heat your plate(s) and place 2 croûtes on each, then pour round them a thin layer of the moderately thick sauce. Stir into the sauce about half a teaspoon of softened *tapenade aux olives* (olive paste) making any design you fancy so that it looks attractive. Perch one black olive in the centre on the top of each cheesed croûte and serve.

An alternative to the olive paste is to use about 10 or 12 very finely crushed capers and to place one caper in the centre on top of each cheesed croûte.

Or you could place a slice of tomato on top of each cheesed croûte and make the pattern in the sauce with a little tomato pureé. You can do this easily if you coat a fork with the tomato pureé or you could use your finger!

Or you could place half an anchovy slice on the top and use some anchovy pureé for making the pattern (again using a fork).

13

PUDDINGS

BREAD AND BUTTER PUDDING

Serve this dish hot. However, it is delicious served cold
and is a great favourite of mine. You can keep any left-
over pudding for 3 days in a cold place (i.e. the
refrigerator).

For this recipe you need 2 or 3 thick slices of stale white
bread. If your bread is fresh, cut the slices at breakfast
time and leave them out in the kitchen to dry out.

Preparation time: 20 minutes.   Cooking time: 40 minutes.

Butter for greasing and spreading
2 or 3 slices stale white bread
1 dessertspn marmalade (optional)
1 tablespn sultanas
1 egg
1 dessertspn/15g/½ oz caster sugar
300ml/½ pint milk
Sprinkle of nutmeg

Pre-heat the oven on gas 4 (350°F/180°C).

Grease well with butter the sides and base of a 600ml/
1 pint oven-proof pie dish.

Butter the bread. I also like to spread it with a little good
quality medium-cut marmalade (not the orange or silver
shred type). Remove the crusts, then cut the bread into
2.5cm/1″ strips or squares.

Cover the base of the dish with the buttered bread
(buttered-side-up) and sprinkle over about a third of the
sultanas, add a second layer of bread and sprinkle over
half the remaining sultanas, then add the final third layer

of bread and sprinkle the rest of the sultanas on top.

Beat the egg with a fork and mix in the sugar, then add the milk, stir it well and pour the mixture over the top of the bread. Grate the nutmeg on top. Place the dish one shelf down from the top of the pre-heated oven and cook for 35–40 minutes until the top bread is slightly browned.

If you like the bread on the top of the pudding to be extra sweet and tasty, sprinkle a dessertspoon of brown sugar over it and place under a hot grill for 4–5 minutes.

BAKED RICE PUDDING

This is a very popular, simple-to-make dish. You can eat it with stewed apples, plums and prunes or with a variety of jams.

It is also easy to reheat or, if you wish, can be eaten cold. Store left-over rice pudding in a cold place (i.e. the refrigerator). Mix it in a basin with an extra dessertspoon of milk and reheat it on gas 4 (350°F/180°C) for about 20 minutes and serve it hot with 2 dessertspoons of jam to your liking.

Preparation time: 5 minutes.
                    Cooking time: 2 hours 15 minutes.

3 teaspns (approx.) butter for greasing
3 level dessertspns/40g/1½ oz Carolina rice
2 dessertspns/25g/1 oz caster sugar
600ml/1 pint (just under) milk
Sprinkle of nutmeg

Pre-heat the oven on gas 4 (350°F/180°C).

Grease with butter the base and sides of a 600ml/1 pint oven-proof dish. Put the rice into a small sieve and wash it well under the cold tap, then pour it into the dish. Sprinkle over the sugar and add just under 600ml/1 pint of milk. (I don't use the whole 600ml/pint as it is liable to spill when placing the dish in the oven.) Cover the top of the milk with nutmeg powder.

Cook for 2 hours on the middle shelf of the pre-heated oven. Some types of rice cook more quickly than other varieties. If you like your pudding milky, it may be sufficiently cooked after 1¾ hours, so test it with a fork. But if you prefer the pudding more solid you may need to cook it for longer than 2 hours.

APPLE CHARLOTTE

Serve on a hot plate with single cream or custard. The latter is easy to make. Buy a small tin of custard powder and follow the instructions on it.

Preparation time: 20 minutes. *Cooking time: 45 minutes.*

2 heaped dessertspns/25g/1 oz butter
2 slices of small white loaf
1 large/225g/8 oz Bramley apple
Juice and grated rind of ½ lemon
4 heaped dessertspns/50g/2 oz caster sugar
¼ teaspn cinnamon
4 cloves
2 tablespns/50g/2 oz breadcrumbs
1 dessertspn demerara sugar

Pre-heat the oven on gas 6 (400°F/200°C).

Grease a 600ml/1 pint sized oven-proof dish with butter. Butter the bread, remove the crusts and line the base and the sides of the dish with the bread.

Peel, core and slice the apple. Stew it over a medium heat with the lemon juice, grated rind, caster sugar, cinnamon and cloves for about 6 minutes. Then squash the mixture with a fork.

Pour the mashed apple into the breaded dish and cover with the breadcrumbs. Sprinkle over the demerara sugar. Dot a few spots of butter over the top.

Put the dish into the pre-heated oven and cook for 45 minutes when the top should be nicely brown.

SPONGE PUDDING WITH JAM

Serve this with custard (follow the instructions on the tin of custard powder) or, as I prefer, with fresh cream.

Preparation time: 12 minutes.　　Cooking time: 30 minutes.

2 level tablespns/50g/2 oz butter
2 tablespns/50g/2 oz caster sugar
1 egg
50g/2 oz self raising flour
½ teaspn cinnamon
3 dessertspns milk
1 teaspn lemon juice
100g/4 oz jam

Pre-heat the oven on gas 4 (350°F/180°C).

Cream the butter and sugar until light and fluffy, either in an electric mixer or with a fork. Beat the egg. Season the flour with the cinnamon and add this to the egg a little at a time, then also add the milk and lemon juice slowly. Mix this with the creamed butter and sugar so that it is moist enough to fall off a spoon.

Grease an oven-proof basin with a little extra butter and put the jam into the bottom, then scoop the mixture on top and smooth it level. Place the basin into the pre-heated oven and bake for 30 minutes until the pudding has risen nicely.

GINGER SPONGE

Prepare as above but omit the jam and add 2 teaspoons of ground ginger to the mixture instead. Also use brown sugar instead of the white caster sugar and, if available, add a dessertspoon of dark rum.

SPOTTED DICK

Prepare as for Sponge Pudding but omit the jam and add 50–75g/2–3 oz mixed dried fruit (sultanas, currants and raisins) to the mixture instead.

PANCAKES

This recipe makes 2 good-sized pancakes. Unfilled pancakes can be frozen for up to 4 months. Stack them one on top of another with greaseproof paper between each layer and wrap them in a freezer bag.

Preparation time: 12 minutes
plus 1 hour resting in the fridge.
Cooking time: 2½ minutes for each pancake.

100g/4 oz flour
Pinch of salt
1 egg
150ml/¼ pint milk
1 teaspn sunflower oil

To make the batter, put the flour into a basin, add a pinch of salt and mix. Break the egg into the flour, add a tablespoon of milk and mix thoroughly into a thickish batter, pouring in and mixing the rest of the milk. Beat well and leave for 1 hour in a cold place (i.e. the refrigerator) before use. During this cooling period it will probably thicken so you may have to add a little more milk, but not too much as you don't want the mixture too thin.

Take a shallow non-stick frying pan with a diameter of 25cm/10″. Smear the oil all over its surface with a finger or a pastry brush. Place over a gentle heat and when it starts to smoke pour in the cooled batter to cover the base thinly and cook for 2 or 3 minutes until it is slightly brown. Turn the pancake over (if you are skilled you may like to toss it!) and fry the other side for a minute. It is then ready to serve on a hot plate.

If you want a lemon pancake, sprinkle the pancake with sugar and a squeeze of lemon. Fold it over, sugar it again and it's ready to eat.

VARIATIONS
You can fill a pancake with jam, sultanas, chopped dates or honey. Or you can fold in diced cooked ham or minced cooked chicken to make a savoury main course pancake. In fact you can add almost whatever you like to a pancake!

BAKED APPLE

This is a popular way to enjoy an apple. You need a large Bramley or other type of cooking apple. Core it and fill its cored centre with a mixture of sultanas and brown sugar. Place it in a baking tin with a small amount of boiling water poured into the base. Put it on a shelf below the centre of a pre-heated oven on gas 2 (300°F/150°C) and cook for 1–1½ hours.

STEWED APPLES

Stewed apples go nicely with Baked Rice Pudding (see page 140).

You need a good cooking apple, such as a Bramley. Peel, core and cut it into slices. Then put it into a saucepan with about a tablespoon of water and a tablespoon of brown sugar per apple. Bring to the boil and simmer until soft but try to keep the slices whole; 10–15 minutes should be ample time. When cooked, place into a serving dish and sprinkle over 1 or 2 teaspoons of cinnamon and sugar if required.

BANANA WITH CREAM

This makes a tasty dessert. Peel a banana and cut it into 5mm/¼" rounds. Place these on a plate and cover with a tablespoon of chopped stoned dates. Pour over 2 tablespoons of thick cream, then sprinkle over the top a tablespoonful of chopped nuts.

ICE CREAM WITH KIWI FRUIT

This only takes 5 minutes to prepare but should be artistically presented on a shallow soup plate or a small bowl with a flat base of about 11cm–12.5cm/4½"–5" diameter.

Skin a kiwi fruit. Slice it thinly, cutting horizontally widthways across the fruit, not lengthways. Arrange the slices in a circle on the base of the plate or bowl leaving a gap in the centre.

Then take a chocolate-covered ice cream which you can buy individually wrapped in cartons from most superstores (these are usually about 8.5cm by 3.5cm/3½" by 1½"), cut it in half (preferably at an angle) and stand one half in the centre of the kiwi fruit circle. Serve with a pompadour fan wafer biscuit. You can put the other half of the ice cream back into the freezer or, if you prefer, use it all. With a guest, it is more attractive to use half each.

MELON SURPRISE

This dish is better served as a dessert than a starter. You need to use a round melon such as a cantaloup or ogen.

Cut the melon in half, remove the seeds and scoop out all the pulp and cut it into roundish balls, keeping the empty shells. Next sprinkle a little sugar into the shells, then mix the melon balls with 3 or 4 strawberries (cut into quarters), a chopped apricot or two, a few raspberries and blackcurrants. Put this fruit mix back into the empty shells with a little more soft sugar and a tablespoon of port or sweet sherry. Cover and place in a refrigerator for about an hour and serve.

FRUIT SALAD

To make a good fruit salad you need to prepare a syrup. You can use fruits in season or whatever is available to make a total weight of about 450g/1 lb, but try and include a minimum of three different fruits. The fruit needs to be cut into bitesize pieces and tossed in the dish or bowl in which you serve it. The quantity this recipe makes will be more than you need for yourself alone but the salad will keep for many weeks or months in the freezer; make sure, however, that you don't include bananas until just before serving.

Preparation time: 15 minutes approx.
plus 1 hour marinating.
Cooking time: 10 minutes.

Various fruit
300ml/½ pint water
100g/4 oz granulated sugar
1 tablespn orange-flavoured liqueur (e.g. Cointreau) or Calvados (optional)
Cream, as much as you like

Place the fruit of your choice into a serving bowl or dish.

To make the syrup, pour the water and the sugar into a small saucepan and boil it for about 10 minutes. For extra flavour, add a tablespoon of the alcohol (if your fruit includes oranges, add the orange-flavoured liqueur; if it includes apples, add the Calvados). When the syrup is cool, pour it over the fruit and leave for 1 hour, stirring occasionally, so that the fruit marinates in the liquid. It is then ready to serve with a little cream if you wish.

FRUIT FOOL

This is another simple way to make a dessert. This recipe makes enough for 2 helpings or to serve 2 people. It can be served warm or cold from the refrigerator.

You can use any fruit you like or a mixture of such fruit as raspberries, blackcurrants, redcurrants, blackberries and strawberries.

Preparation time: 15 minutes.   *Cooking time: 10 minutes.*

225g/½ lb mixed fruit
1 tablespn water
1 tablespn granulated sugar
300ml/½ pint custard (follow the instructions on the tin of custard powder)

Put the fruit, water and sugar into a saucepan and cook over a moderate heat for 5 or 6 minutes until soft.

When the custard is prepared, pour it into the fruit mixture and beat with a fork or use a food processor to make it nicely smooth.

14

ENTERTAINING

Here are some recipes for tasty dishes for you to serve when entertaining a friend. Each feeds two people.

CURRIED BEEF   *Serves two.*

Serve the beef on a hot plate surrounded with the cooked rice and enjoy it with a glass of beer or red wine.

You can buy a tin of pre-cooked rice. You can heat it up while finishing cooking the meat; it only takes 3 minutes to make hot.

Preparation time: 15 minutes.   Cooking time: 40 minutes.

225g/8 oz beefsteak (rump)
2 level tablespns/50g/2 oz butter
1 small onion (peeled and finely chopped)
½ large cooking apple (peeled and chopped)
2 dessertspns curry powder
2 dessertspns sultanas
Seasoning: salt and pepper
1 teaspn garlic granules
1 teaspn flour

(continued overleaf)

(Curried Beef continued)

1 beef stock cube
1½ cups water
½ teaspn caster sugar
1 teaspn garam masala
2 tablespn cooked rice

Cut the beefsteak into small cubes. Melt the butter in a lidded saucepan or large frying pan over a medium heat and add the beef cubes. Cook on a medium heat for about 5 minutes, turning the meat until it is brown all over. Add the onion, apple, curry powder, sultanas, salt, pepper and garlic.

Meanwhile, put the flour into a large cup. Dissolve the beef stock cube in a dessertspoon of water and pour this slowly onto the flour and mix it into a paste, gradually adding and mixing in the rest of the water. Pour this into the meat mixture and stir in the sugar. Cook for a further 12 minutes, continuing to stir to prevent it burning.

Put the lid on and cook for 15 minutes over a simmering heat until the beef is tender. Five minutes before serving, add the garam masala. Then serve with the rice.

MEAT BALLS IN TOMATO SAUCE *Serves two*

A warming recipe for the colder weather.

Preparation time: 15 minutes.   *Cooking time: 1 hour.*

½ medium-sized onion
225g/8 oz minced beef
1 tablespn chopped parsley
½ teaspn mixed dried herbs (obtainable in a small carton)
Seasoning: salt and pepper
1 egg
½ cup flour
2 tablespns sunflower oil

Peel, cut and finely chop the half onion. Mix it in a bowl with the beef, parsley, herbs, salt and pepper. Beat the egg and add to the mixture and stir it into a sticky consistency.

Scoop out a generous dessertspoon of the mixture onto a floured plate, then with floured hands roll it into a small ball with a diameter of about 1.5cm/¾". Repeat with the rest of the mixture.

Heat the oil in a frying pan over a medium heat and add the balls. Keep turning them over until all their surfaces are well browned. Remove them from the pan and put to one side, preferably placing them onto absorbent kitchen paper so that they can drain. Then put them into a casserole dish and leave on one side while you make the tomato sauce.

Pre-heat the oven on gas 4 (350°F/180°C).

TOMATO SAUCE
Preparation time: 15 minutes.

1 (227g/8 oz) tin of tomatoes
1 dessertspn cornflour
1 dessertspn tomato purée
1 teaspn garlic granules (or crushed clove of garlic)
Seasoning: pepper

Open the tin of tomatoes and strain them into a basin. Retain the juice and mix the cornflour into it gradually so that you don't get any lumps. Then stir this into the drained tomatoes in the basin.

Now refill the empty tomato tin with water, add the tomato purée and mix well. Add this to the tomato mixture with the garlic granules and pepper.

Pour this sauce over the meat balls in the casserole dish. Put into the pre-heated oven and cook for 1 hour.

PAM'S CORONATION CHICKEN   *Serves two.*

This recipe was given to me by a friend. It makes an enjoyable meal for a summer evening. Drink a glass or two of the red wine with it and follow it with a dessert of ice cream or fruit.

Serve the chicken on a bed of cooked rice. For this, you can use pre-cooked tinned rice which only takes 3 minutes to heat, after which you can allow it to cool. Or see page 66.

The advantage of this recipe is that you can prepare it the day before and keep it covered in the refrigerator.

Preparation time: 10 minutes plus 15 minutes cooling.
Cooking time: 15 minutes.

½ medium-size onion
1 medium-size carrot
1 stalk of celery
2 chicken breasts
3 peppercorns
½ teaspn salt
1 bouquet garni (on sale in small bags)
1 chicken stock cube
425ml/¾ pint water

Peel, cut and finely chop the onion. Clean and chop the carrot and celery. Put the chicken breasts into a lidded saucepan with the onion, carrot, celery, peppercorns, salt and a sachet of bouquet garni. Dissolve the stock cube into the water and pour this into the saucepan so that it covers all the ingredients. Bring to the boil, put the lid on and simmer for 15 minutes. Meanwhile, prepare the Curry Mayonnaise, as below.

Turn off the heat, leave to cool in the pan for about 15 minutes, then cut the chicken into bite-size pieces.

CURRY MAYONNAISE
While the chicken is cooking, you have plenty of time to make the sauce which is an essential part of this dish.

Preparation time: 10 minutes.   Cooking time: 10 minutes.

1 small onion
1 dessertspn sunflower oil
1 teaspn curry powder (I prefer Madras)
1 tablespn tomato purée

(continued overleaf)

(Pam's Coronation Chicken continued)

1 tablespn water
2 tablespns red wine
1 tablespn apricot jam
1 cup/25g/1 oz mayonnaise

Peel, cut and finely chop the onion, put it into a frying pan with the oil and cook until soft over a medium heat (about 5 minutes). Add the curry powder and cook for a further 2 minutes. Then dilute the tomato purée in the water and add to the pan with the red wine, simmering the mixture for a further 3 minutes. Then stir in the jam. Leave to cool, then rub through a strainer with the back of a wooden spoon (or liquidise in an electric blender) into a basin and stir in the mayonnaise.

Pour the sauce over the chicken pieces, turning them to ensure they are all well covered with the sauce.

PORK CHINESE-STYLE *Serves two.*

This makes an attractive and enjoyable meal for two.

Use pre-cooked tinned rice which only takes 3 minutes to heat up and so is quickly ready to serve with the pork. Beanshoots go well with this dish. You can buy them in packets; they only take 6 minutes to cook.

Preparation time: 15 minutes.   Cooking time: 30 minutes.

1 dessertspn/10g/¼ oz butter
1 tablespn sunflower oil
4 oz/100g diced pork
½ green pepper
1 tomato
6 spring onions
Seasoning: salt and pepper
½ cup sherry
1 tablespn soy sauce
2 level dessertspns pre-cooked rice

Heat the butter and oil in a shallow saucepan over a medium heat, then add the pork pieces and cook for 10 minutes, turning from time to time.

Remove and discard the seeds from the pepper, chop the pepper into fairly small pieces and add to the partly cooked pork, cooking for another 5 minutes.

Peel and chop the tomato. Chop the spring onions, using the first 5cm/2" of the green stem and discarding the rest. Season well. Add the tomato and spring onions with the sherry to the pork and cook for a further 5 minutes.

Pour the soy sauce over the rice while it is being warmed up.

KEDGEREE   *Serves two.*

Some people like this dish for breakfast but I prefer it as a
main course in the evening.

You can cook the haddock earlier in the day by boiling it
in a dessertspoon each of milk and water for about 6
minutes. Drain it, remove the skin and flake the fish
roughly.

Preparation time: 15 minutes.   Cooking time: 25 minutes.

2 eggs
4 level tablespns/100g/4 oz cooked tinned rice
1 teaspn turmeric powder
2 level dessertspns/15g/½ oz butter
½ small onion (finely chopped)
100g/4 oz cooked smoked haddock (flaked)
Seasoning: salt and cayenne pepper
½ teaspn paprika
½ cup single cream (or natural yoghurt)
1 dessertspn parsley (finely chopped)

Hard boil the eggs (see page 37); this will take 8 minutes.
Place them into cold water, remove their shells and chop
them into 16 small pieces.

Heat the rice in a little water for 3 minutes as instructed
on the can so that the rice absorbs the water. Stir in the
turmeric.

In a frying pan, melt the butter over a medium heat, add
the onion and fry for about 7 or 8 minutes until it is soft
but not brown. Then scatter the haddock into the pan and
continue heating for another 5 minutes. Next add the egg,
season the rice with the salt, cayenne pepper and paprika

and add to the mixture. Stir over a moderate heat for 5 minutes and mix in the cream or yoghurt.

Serve on a hot plate and sprinkle the chopped parsley to your liking.

PRAWNS WITH ALMONDS   *Serves two.*

This is a special dish and it takes time to prepare. These large prawns are delicious, they are not cheap but it is nice to have them as a treat now and again, especially if you are entertaining a friend or relative. All you need with this are 12 new potatoes boiled with a sprig or two of mint.

Preparation time: 20 minutes.   Cooking time: 30 minutes.

8 prawns (Dublin Bay or Mediterranean)
1½ cups water
25g/1 oz almond pieces
Seasoning: salt and pepper
1 level dessertspn/10g/¼ oz butter
½ cup white wine
1 dessertspn double cream

First remove the heads and shells from the prawns (this is rather fiddly). Then put the heads and shells into a saucepan with the water. Put on the lid and boil gently for 20 minutes or longer. The object is to obtain all the flavour and colour from the heads/shells to make a sauce.

You may have to add more water because it is necessary to end up after the cooking with about 1 cup of juices.

Next, grind the almond pieces quite small but not into

powder. This only takes a minute in a food mixer.

Take out the heads and shells from the boiling water and throw them away, then pour the remaining liquid into a frying pan. Add the ground almonds, salt and pepper, stir and heat it. Melt in the butter. When it's all mixed in, add the skinned prawns and the white wine and cook for about 5 minutes, turning the fish from time to time.

Remove the prawns onto a hot dish or onto 2 hot plates. Add the cream to the sauce, heat it and serve poured round the prawns.

INDEX